"This is the book you'll want to take on your
when it's not being carted around in a satche
idence on your lifelong spiritual contempla'

"I highly recommend."

—Martin E. Marty, *Context*

"For more than 40 years, William Sloane Coffin has both enraptured and
challenged the nation with his vibrant calls for peace and social justice.
Even absent Coffin's extraordinary instrument—his peerless preacher's
voice—the passionate music of his ministry soars from these pages."

—Garry Trudeau, creator of the comic strip *Doonesbury*

"If you are young, you may never have heard of this man. But if you are of a
certain age, you probably remember him well. For many he was a hero . . ."

—Bob Abernathy, on the PBS broadcast *Religion and Ethics Newsweekly*

"Bill Coffin's eloquent and prophetic voice and indomitable spirit abound
in this inspiring book. They will enrich and strengthen our lives and those
of generations to come. What a gift Coffin's wisdom is to us all."

— Marian Wright Edelman, President, Children's Defense Fund

"A stirring compendium of 'Coffiniana.' I myself, knowing him well, find
Credo to be 'the essential Bill Coffin,' the Coffin to remember. I shall treasure its inspiration always."

—H. Bradford Westerfield, Professor Emeritus
at Yale University, *Yale Alumni Magazine*

"William Sloane Coffin is a towering prophet in our day. His perennial
wisdom and courageous actions exemplify the best of Christian witness."

—Cornel West

"*Credo* overflows with passion, incisive thinking, imaginative political
insights, and prophetic calls for action. . . . May we all know and experience
more of this kind of good religion in the months and years to come."

—*Spirituality and Health*

"The best of Coffin's words from his extraordinarily un-boring life."

—*Publishers Weekly's Religion BookLine*

"Those who encounter this magnificent *Credo* will quickly realize it is a
work of love of the highest order."

—*Circuit Rider*

CREDO

William Sloane Coffin

WJK WESTMINSTER
JOHN KNOX PRESS
LOUISVILLE · KENTUCKY

Cover design by designpointinc.com
Author photo by Robert Shetterly

First paperback edition
Published by Westminster John Knox Press
Louisville, Kentucky

This book is printed on acid-free paper that meets the American National Standards Institute Z39.48 standard.

PRINTED IN THE UNITED STATES OF AMERICA

06 07 08 09 10 11 12 13 — 10 9 8 7 6 5 4 3

Library of Congress Cataloging-in-Publication Data
A catalog record for this book is available from the Library of Congress.
ISBN-13: 978-0-664-22948-1
ISBN-10: 0-664-22948-4

To my beloved wife Randy

Te adoro.

Contents

Foreword

James Carroll

A steel wall separated your cramped space from that of the man in the adjoining cell of the D.C. lock-up. It was an overnight incarceration after being arrested for trespassing at the U.S. Capitol. The year was 1972. In the cell block, in separate cells, were another two dozen or so prisoners who had been part of your anti-war protest. Unlike those of many demonstrations, yours was a relatively timid group, made up mainly of ministers and priests—"religious leaders"—and the night was passing with anguished slowness. Murmurs occasionally broke the silence, and doors clanged on a distant corridor. The barked orders of guards jolted the air now and then. Otherwise, an eerie stillness filled the dark.

You yourself, a man raised to revere authority and obey it, were entirely disoriented to find yourself a lawbreaker. You were depressed and afraid. Even now, when you think of the Dark Night of the Soul, you think of the chill of that steel wall against your shoulder. And you think of that feeling—a steady sinking— you yourself the stone falling in the well of your own chest.

Even now you have no idea what prompted him to do so, but at some point in that night, the man in the next cell began to sing, softly at first. His resolute baritone gradually filled the air as he moved easily into the lyric of what you soon recognized as Handel's *Messiah:* "Comfort ye, comfort ye my people." And then you recognized the voice as that of William Sloane Coffin, the most familiar voice in the group. He had been the putative spokesman at the Capitol demonstration, the voice of an ad hoc community, saying you would not leave the great rotunda until Congress voted an end to the war. Fat chance.

Now Coffin sang as if he were alone on the earth, and the old words rose through the dark as if Isaiah himself had returned to speak for you to God—to speak for God to you. Others in the cell block soon joined their voices to Coffin's—"The people that walked in darkness have seen a great light"—but his voice, in effect, carried the others. He knew the words, and he knew the music.

You yourself, suffering a Roman Catholic's ignorance both of the Scriptures and of great choral art, remained mute. But your silence, too, was swept into what had become nothing less than prayer. As you listened to Coffin—"All we like sheep, all we like sheep, all we like sheep—have gone astray"—you suddenly felt awash in an unexpected gratitude, for you realized that those words expressed your deepest faith, and that sung as they were, those words had an absolute integrity that far transcended your fearful hesitance. You *did* believe that your Redeemer liveth, and, more than that, you believed that your Redeemer had stood upon the earth with you, bringing you to that most unlikely place. You saw, indeed, that you belonged there, in that cell block, and that you were plenty strong enough for whatever lay ahead.

That night, in a way that was unprecedented, you experienced the demanding yet consoling force of your most deeply held conviction: God exists. God exists for all. God exists for you. Yet until then, you had not known it. The sacred words of Isaiah, Job, the psalmist, Paul, and the author of Revelation, together with the genius of Handel—"Alleluia, for the Lord God omnipotent . . ."— were all mediated through the human eloquence of William Sloane Coffin, who, through expression rooted in his own person, made the mystery present. For a moment, you believed in God— ". . . reign for ever and ever"—because William Sloane Coffin did.

As you felt his music vibrate the steel at your shoulder, you believed in yourself, too, because he did. "Amen."

Bill Coffin was a stranger to you then—an admired figure whom you had sought to emulate—but years later you would become friends. The intimacy of your mutual and deep affection never dulled the force of what had initially made you admire him so. In the early 1960s, he came to the Washington seminary where you were preparing for the priesthood. Already famous as the chaplain at Yale, where he served from 1958 to 1975, he was a figure—perhaps *the* figure—of white alliance with the black movement for full equality.

You will never forget his stirring sermon that day. You say "sermon," though his talk was billed as a lecture, and he spoke from a lectern in an auditorium because Catholics and Protestants still did not gather at pulpits together. Yet the sermon is Coffin's form, and what he did that day, with corduroy jacket and work boots for vestments, was nothing if not preach. There was the trademark pithiness, the rhetorical sophistication, the erudite citations, and, above all, the Scriptures as a native language. But what really stunned you and your fellow Thomists—you were being trained in syllogisms—was the unbridled passion with which Coffin announced his gospel.

And what a gospel it was. The world he described was upside-down: the church on the side of the poor; the powerful at risk for losing everything; the disenfranchised as sole custodians of moral legitimacy. Coffin, in his passionate sermon that day, was perhaps the first person from which you heard that defining question: Whose side are you on? Your answer would be the nearly ten years in coming that it took for you to go to jail—and wouldn't Coffin, by pure coincidence, be in the next cell, with that song to say welcome home?

Coincidence? No. Such is the Providence around which William Sloane Coffin builds his ministry. Eventually, you would understand that William Sloane Coffin has spun a thousand webs of such seemingly random connection. A legion of men and women has discovered themselves in his words, in his example, in his story. A child of the establishment, he became a tribune of America's outcasts. A man with a warrior's mettle—and a spy's entrée—he responded to the massive militarization of his beloved nation by becoming its most widely heard voice of peace. A college chaplain, he changed both how colleges think of themselves and what chaplains dare to undertake.

You yourself, once you were ordained, applied for a chaplain's job so that you could model yourself on him. You got the job and did so—right down to the corduroy jacket and work boots.

There are many ways to understand the unprecedented reach of William Sloane Coffin's influence. Some emphasize the golden ticket with which he was born, gaining him admission to the most elite circles of religion, society, and politics. When one so clearly of its own challenges the establishment, it listens.

Others emphasize the authority Coffin earned for himself—security clearances, expertise in Russian, the Cold War's most valued credentials of *realpolitic*. The context of such youthful arrival to a position of high influence and responsibility shifted dramatically when Coffin then put his courage to the test—and proved it—in a series of dangerous confrontations during the deep-South civil rights struggle, and then in the high-risk legal challenge he mounted in resistance to an illegal war. At a crucial moment, he helped turn America back toward its truest self.

Some emphasize Coffin's role as the prophet of a new way of being religious, as he left behind the absolutes of narrow denominationalism to forge a far deeper and more lasting connection based on the one commandment of love that undergirds each of the great religions—none more than Christianity. Yet Coffin has never been more a Protestant than in refusing to yield the language of religion—his native tongue those Scriptures—to the ascendant Religious Right in late twentieth century and early twenty-first century America. In that he has become, just by being there, an organizing center for a new kind of religious affiliation. And in this arc of his own story—from activist ministry at Williams and Yale, to the national pulpit of Riverside Church, to honed opposition to nuclear weapons at SANE-FREEZE, to his lecturing, teaching, and preaching since—many see the ultimate vindication of the idea that religious faith requires political commitment. Love and Justice are mates. God and the world are one.

All of these themes go a long way toward explaining the momentous impact of William Sloane Coffin on his generation, his nation, and his church. But there is one element that serves as the engine driving all these turbines, the thing that distinguishes Coffin's contribution and sets it above the good works of others. And that is the extraordinary eloquence of Coffin's language. This book is a feast of rare expression, a display of subtlety and insight that shows why Bill Coffin matters so much to America and the world. The economy of verbal construction, the wit, the grasp of the core, the biblical ground, the high literateness, the knack for simplicity, the infallible feel for the memorable word, and the sly understanding of the uses of irony—all joined to the convictions that God exists and that God's existence matters—make Bill Coffin the greatest public preacher of his time.

The good words collected here, drawing from the treasures of what Coffin has said in a thousand circumstances, serve, also, as a kind of chronicle of the things that matter most in the early twenty-first century: how lovers are together; how a nation fends off the temptation to empire; how peace can be organized after all; how grief defines happiness; how God lives on this beleaguered earth. On these pages, readers will find insights that ring with originality and freshness, and at the same time give expression to the very things one has always felt. And in making palpable such precious hopes, William Sloane Coffin manages something else that seems impossible—he performs virtuoso feats of articulation without drawing attention to himself. Here is the persistent wonder: that this gifted, exceptionally gracious, large-hearted man is so deeply humble. It is as if he has no idea how beautiful his expression is, how impressive his grasp of the Word, how desperately needed is his voice. How once heard, it is not to be forgotten.

This book is a treasure because with it you can tell William Sloane Coffin what he has meant to you, and how you love him.

And it is a treasure because it enables the words of William Sloane Coffin that have already changed a nation, rescued a legion, and praised the Lord to go on doing so long after all of us, in the mystery of God's loving plan, are gone.

Preface

C redo—I believe—best translates "I have given my heart to." However imperfectly, I have given my heart to the teaching and example of Christ, which, among many other things, informs my understanding of faiths other than Christianity.

Certainly religions are different. Still most seek to fulfill the same function; that is, they strive to convert people from self-preoccupation to the wholehearted giving of oneself in love for God and for others. To love God by loving neighbor is an impulse equally at the heart of Christianity, Judaism, and Islam. It therefore makes eminent sense in today's fractured world for religious people to move from truth-claiming to the function truth plays.

Moreover, when we consider how, on a whole range of questions—from the number of sacraments to the ordination of women, pacifism, abortion, and homosexuality—Christians cannot arrive at universal agreement, then we have to be impressed by a divine incomprehensibility so vast that no human being dare speak for the Almighty. As St. Paul asks, "For who has known the mind of God?" To learn from one another and to work together towards common goals of justice and peace—this surely is what suffering humanity has every right to expect of believers of all faiths.

The idea for this book came from publisher Davis Perkins, who asked editor Stephanie Egnotovich to look over a lifetime of sermons and my unpublished speeches, then to excerpt from them paragraphs and sentences to be organized into rough categories. Stephanie basically did the work; I had only to add a little bit here, delete a little bit there. Seldom has an author owed so much to an editor.

The book is designed to be read slowly and in no particular order. The separate paragraphs reflect conclusions I have reached during a lifetime of continuous education. Now that my years appear to be hastening to their end, I want to acknowledge how much I owe my many, many teachers. Believe me, a totally original idea is a remarkable rarity!

Finally, I like to believe that I am an American patriot who loves his country enough to address her flaws. Today these are many, and all preachers worth their salt need fearlessly to insist that "God 'n' country" is not one word.

—WILLIAM SLOANE COFFIN

Faith, Hope, Love

And now faith, hope, and love abide,
these three; and the
greatest of these is love.
                              —1 Cor. 13:13

Jesus thou art all compassion
Pure unbounded love thou art
Visit us with thy salvation
Enter every trembling heart.
                              —Charles Wesley

ocrates had it wrong; it is not the unexamined but finally the uncommitted life that is not worth living. Descartes too was mistaken; "Cogito ergo sum"—"I think therefore I am"? Nonsense. "Amo ergo sum"—"I love therefore I am." Or, as with unconscious eloquence St. Paul wrote, "Now abide faith, hope, love, these three; and the greatest of these is love."

I believe that. I believe it is better not to live than not to love.

———— ⤜ ————

Make love your aim, not biblical inerrancy, nor purity nor obedience to holiness codes. Make love your aim, for

"Though I speak with the tongues of men and of angels"— musicians, poets, preachers, you are being addressed;

"and though I . . . understand all mysteries, and all knowledge"—professors, your turn,

"and though I bestow all my goods to feed the poor"—radicals take note;

"and though I give my body to be burned"—the very stuff of heroism;

"and have not charity, it profiteth me nothing" (1 Cor. 13:1–3 KJV).

I doubt if in any other scriptures of the world there is a more radical statement of ethics. If we fail in love, we fail in all things else.

—— ⤳ ——

And if we are not yet one in love at least we are one in sin, which is no mean bond because it precludes the possibility of separation through judgment.

—— ⤳ ——

Of God's love we can say two things: it is poured out universally for everyone from the Pope to the loneliest wino on the planet; and secondly, God's love doesn't seek value, it creates value. It is not because we have value that we are loved, but because we are loved that we have value. Our value is a gift, not an achievement.

—— ⤳ ——

Because our value is a gift, we don't have to prove ourselves, only to express ourselves, and what a world of difference there is between proving ourselves and expressing ourselves.

—— ⤳ ——

We don't have to be "successful," only valuable. We don't have to make money, only a difference, and particularly in the lives society counts least and puts last.

--- ⚜ ---

It is terribly important to realize that the leap of faith is not so much a leap of thought as of action. For while in many matters it is first we must see, then we will act; in matters of faith it is first we must do then we will know, first we will be and then we will see. One must, in short, dare to act wholeheartedly without absolute certainty.

--- ⚜ ---

I love the recklessness of faith. First you leap, and then you grow wings.

--- ⚜ ---

What is faith? Faith is being grasped by the power of love. Faith is recognizing that what makes God is infinite mercy, not infinite control; not power, but love unending. Faith is recognizing that if at Christmas Jesus became like us, it was so that we might become more like him. We know what that means: watching Jesus heal the sick, empower the poor, and scorn the powerful, we see transparently the power of God at work. Watching Zaccheus climb the tree a crook and come down a saint, watching Paul set out a hatchet man for the Pharisees and return a fool for Christ, we know that our lives too can become channels for divine mercy to flow out to save the lost and the suffering.

―――― ≋ ――――

There is nothing anti-intellectual in the leap of faith, for faith is not believing without proof but trusting without reservation. Faith is no substitute for thinking. On the contrary, it is what makes good thinking possible. It has what we might call a limbering effect on the mind; by taking us beyond familiar ground, faith ends up giving us that much more to think about. Certainly Peter and Andrew and James and John, in deciding to follow Jesus, received more to think about than had they stayed at home. And so it is with all of us: if we give our lives to Christ, if we leave familiar territory and take the leap of faith, what we receive in return fills our minds altogether as much as it fills our hearts.

―――― ≋ ――――

The first of the four cardinal virtues of the Roman Catholic Church is "prudentia," which basically means damn good thinking. Christ came to take away our sins, not our minds.

―――― ≋ ――――

Spirituality means to me living the ordinary life extraordinarily well.

As the old church father said, "The glory of God is a human being fully alive."

------ ≫ ------

We must guard against being too individualistic and elitist in our understanding of spirituality. Some Christians talk endlessly about the importance of one's interior life and how to develop it more fully, forgetting that Christ is born to bring hope and joy also to whole communities of people—the exiles, the deported, the tortured, the silenced.

------ ≫ ------

It is bad religion to deify doctrines and creeds. While indispensable to religious life, doctrines and creeds are only so as signposts. Love alone is the hitching post. Doctrines, let's not forget, supported slavery and apartheid; some still support keeping women in their places and gays and lesbians in limbo. Moreover, doctrines can divide while compassion can only unite. In other words, religious folk, all our lives, have both to recover tradition and to recover *from* it!

------ ≫ ------

The joy that is of God is not opposed to earthly pleasures. Rather it infuses them with a foundation of meaning.

------- ⊰⊱ -------

Miracles do not a messiah make. But a messiah can do miracles. If you ask me if Jesus literally raised Lazarus from the dead, literally walked on water and changed water into wine, I will answer, "For certain, I do not know. But this I do know: faith must be lived before it is understood, and the more it is lived, the more things become possible." I can also report that in home after home I have seen Jesus change beer into furniture, sinners into saints, hate-filled relations into loving ones, cowardice into courage, the fatigue of despair into the buoyancy of hope. In instance after instance, life after life, I have seen Christ be "God's power unto salvation," and that's miracle enough for me.

------- ⊰⊱ -------

All saving ideas are born small. God comes to earth as a child so that we can finally grow up, which means we can stop blaming God for being absent when we ourselves were not present, stop blaming God for the ills of the world as if we had been laboring to cure them, and stop making God responsible for all the thinking and doing we should be undertaking on our own. I've said it before and will probably say it many times again: God provides minimum protection, maximum support—support to help us grow up, to stretch our minds and hearts until they are as wide as God's universe. God doesn't want us narrow-minded, priggish, and subservient, but joyful and loving, as free for one another as God's love was freely poured out for us at Christmas in that babe in the manger.

------- ⊰⊱ -------

Joy is the most important Christian emotion. Duty calls only when gratitude fails to prompt.

───── ⟨⟩ ─────

When Jesus says, "Our Father, who art in heaven," I listen. Even during my doubting days in college I listened, and carefully, because Jesus knew not only more about God than I did—that was obvious; he also knew more about the world. He could talk convincingly to me about a father in heaven because he took seriously the earth's homeless orphans. He could talk to me convincingly about living at peace in the hands of love because he knew that the world lived constantly at war in the grip of hatred. He could talk to me of light, and joy, and exultation, because I knew that he himself knew darkness, sorrow, and death. That's why, eventually, Jesus became for me too my Lord and Savior, and that's why I think it right to say that the authority of the Lord's Prayer stems from the reliability of the source.

───── ⟨⟩ ─────

"Seek ye first the kingdom of God and his righteousness." All well and good; but Christ, who spoke those words, also knows that just as foxes spoil a vineyard, so it is the small carking cares that generally undermine the spiritual foundations of our lives. After all, it was for only thirty pieces of silver, for five newly purchased oxen, for a mess of pottage in an hour of exhaustion, that three biblical characters forfeited their eternal birthright and blessing. And are we not tempted to do the same?

───── ⟨⟩ ─────

Then I saw another thing, that a broken pride does not make for passivity as I had thought. "The world owes me a living"—that's passive. "I owe the world and God a life"—that's active.

⸻ ⥇ ⸻

The consequences of the past are always with us, and half the hostilities tearing the world apart could be resolved today were we to allow the forgiveness of sins to alter these consequences. Let's go further: all the hostilities in our personal and planetary life could be ended were we to allow the forgiveness of sins to act as a lightning rod grounding all these hostilities; if we were to say of ourselves, "The hostility stops here."

⸻ ⥇ ⸻

Jesus is both a mirror to our humanity and a window to divinity, a window revealing as much of God as is given mortal eyes to see. When Christians see Christ empowering the weak, scorning the powerful, healing the wounded, and judging their tormentors, we are seeing transparently the power of God at work. What is finally important is not that Christ is Godlike, but that God is Christ-like. God is like Christ. That's what we need to know, isn't it? Then we know how to pray—"through Jesus Christ, our Lord," who gives us the right and confidence to pray the way we do.

⸻ ⥇ ⸻

We want God to be strong, so that we can be weak. But He wants to be weak so that we can be strong. We want God to prove herself. But she answers, "Do you want proof or freedom?"

----- ⬳ -----

Here we are dealing with another cornerstone of the Christian faith: God is a good father—which is to say, he is not paternalistic. (*Pater noster non est paternalistic!*) As all of us who strive to be good parents know, love is self-restricting when it comes to power. We cannot exercise our power in such fashion as to restrict the freedom of our children— the freedom to become the independent, mature people God meant them to be. Likewise God has left his servants freedom of choice.

----- ⬳ -----

When things go badly in the kingdoms of this world, as invariably they do, given the callous insensibility that turns human beings away from their neighbors in preoccupation with their own troubles, or with dreams of aggrandizement—in such bad moments, many people turn from God, saying, "How could God permit such bad things to happen?" Instead of becoming alienated from their faith in God, wouldn't it make more sense for them to become alienated from their mislaid hopes in human beings, alienated from shallow notions of automatic progress, from sentimental notions about the "nobility of man"? Of course we should love and live for one another. Not, however, because you and I are so lovable, but simply because that's the only way we are going to *become* lovable. Love one another, but *"in God we trust."* You couldn't come up with a phrase more suitable for the coin of a kingdom of this world than "In God we trust."

------ ⊰⊱ ------

What is also important for all people to realize is that what is literally true is insignificant. What is significant is what is eternally true, and it is eternally true of the Bible that its words come to us not as universal precepts for all time to which we must give assent, but as words directed to eternally human situations in which we must decide.

------ ⊰⊱ ------

A Roman Catholic priest and friend said recently, "The Bible is true, and some things happened."

------ ⊰⊱ ------

And Gracie Allen had a strong suggestion: "Never put a period where God has put a comma."

------ ⊰⊱ ------

In the Holy Land are two ancient bodies of water. Both are fed by the Jordan River. In one, fish play and roots find sustenance. In the other, there is no splash of fish, no sound of bird, no leaf around. The difference is not in the Jordan, for it empties into both, but in the Sea of Galilee: for every drop taken in one goes out. It gives and lives. The other gives nothing. And it is called the Dead Sea.

------- ⟨⟩ -------

Strangely enough, it is because we are so passionless that we are so joyless, for passion leads to the springs of gladness. In the book of Hebrews we read, "For the joy that was set before him Jesus endured the cross, despising the shame." The joy is the joy of self-fulfillment. It is also the joy of coming to know God, for knowledge of God is heartfelt, vital. And if God is a suffering God, if this whole universe is borne on a heart infinite in compassion, then the more we suffer in his name the closer we come to him. And the closer we come the more we are convinced that we are loved with a love far more dependable than our own, prized more highly than ever we could prize ourselves, so that like Jesus we can be full of joy, strongly invulnerable in the midst of our vulnerability. That is why to the women weeping along the way of sorrows Jesus said, "Weep for yourselves not for me." To all appearances the incident was closed; love's boat had smashed against the daily grind. But in the eyes of faith all would be finally well.

------- ⟨⟩ -------

If we misconceive God as Father Protector, as one, so to speak, in charge of all the uncontrolled contingencies along the way, then each disappointment reduces what may confidently be affirmed about God. And this is how most people lose their faith.

——— ❧ ———

Perhaps the worst form of psychological pain is the guilt that comes from sin. Some of you may be suffering some terrible guilt for an action you consider unforgivable. But the very word "unforgivable" is itself unforgivable, because it is precisely what can't be condoned that can only be forgiven. Nothing less *needs* forgiveness. Remember also that scars of all sorts are all right. Scars are wounds that have healed, not without a trace, but have healed nonetheless. Think of all the scar tissue around Christ's heart, Jesus our wounded healer.

——— ❧ ———

I don't know why sin is such a bad word. Obviously we're all sinners, the more so the more we try to deny it. But that's not the issue. At issue is whether there is more mercy in God than sin in us. And according to Paul, just as love is stronger than death, so forgiveness is stronger than sin. That may be the hardest thing to believe, for guilt is the last stronghold of pride. "Guilty" represents my opinion of myself. "Forgiven" may represent yours or God's opinion, and I'm too proud to let others do for me what I cannot do for myself. Occasionally it is more blessed to receive than to give. At least it takes more humility.

——— ❧ ———

"There was no room for him in the inn." That phrase, so symbolic of Christ's life, may be as true today as it was two thousand years ago. During Christ's time on earth the only place where there was room for him was in a manger and on the cross. And is there any more room for him today, in our overcrowded hearts, in our cities that can provide only temporary shelters for the homeless, in our nation where planning for nuclear war has become as American as apple pie? It might be more accurate to say that Christ's search for a place to be born, and our rejection of him—the search and the rejection both—go on today as they did then and as they probably always will.

So why are Christians so often so joyless? It is, I think, because too often Christians have only enough religion to make themselves miserable. Guilt they know, but not forgiveness. Nietzsche correctly noted, "Christians should look more redeemed."

One trouble with guilt is that it often seeks punishment in order to avoid judgment; for while judgment demands a new way of life, punishment, by assuaging a bit the guilt, makes the old bearable anew.

Years of being a counselor have enormously increased my suspicion of both guilt and loneliness. I know guilt is hell and that guilty people therefore are deserving of much sympathy. But what I am beginning to suspect is that most guilty people reject the possibility of forgiveness not because it is too good to believe, but because they fear the responsibility forgiveness entails. It's hell to be guilty, but it's worse to be responsible.

As for loneliness, it too has deep roots in selfishness, for its anguish stems less from having no one with whom to share one's burdens, more from having only one's burdens to share.

The banality of guilt is that it is such a convenient substitute for responsibility. It's so much easier to beat your breast than to stick your neck out.

If faith puts us on the road, hope keeps us there.

It's hope that helps us keep the faith, despite the evidence, knowing that only in so doing has the evidence any chance of changing.

———— ⤛⤜ ————

Hope has nothing to do with optimism. Its opposite is not pessimism but despair. And if Jesus never allowed his soul to be cornered into despair, clearly we Christians shouldn't either.

———— ⤛⤜ ————

Hope criticizes what is, hopelessness rationalizes it. Hope resists, hopelessness adapts.

———— ⤛⤜ ————

How often it is that those furthest from the seats of power are nearer to the heart of things. Remember that listening to Jesus, seated on the mountainside were no Roman centurions, no King Herods, no Pharisees. These were ordinary folk, the kind likely as not to stone the prophets, to beg Moses to lead them back to Egypt. Yet it was to them that Jesus said, "You are the salt of the earth"; "You are the light of the world."

Has common humanity ever received so high a compliment from so informed a source?

———— ⤛⤜ ————

One of my favorite stories concerns a beggar in sixteenth-century Paris who, desperately ill, was taken to the operating table of a group of doctors. In Latin, which they were sure he would not understand, the doctors said, "Faciamus experimentum in anima vile" (Let us experiment on this vile fellow). The beggar, who was actually an impoverished student, later to become a renowned poet, Marc Antoine Muret, replied from the slab on which they had laid him, "Animam vilem appellas pro qua Christus non dedignatus mori est?" (Will you call vile one for whom Christ did not disdain to die?).

If Christ did not disdain to die for any of us, who are we not to live for all of us?

———— ⧼ ————

Martin Luther was right: "God can carve the rotten wood and ride the lame horse."

———— ⧼ ————

True, we have to hate evil; else we're sentimental. But if we hate evil more than we love the good, we become damn good haters, and of those the world already has too many. However deep, our anger, like that of Christ, must always and only measure our love.

———— ⧼ ————

What a wonderful thing it would be if once and for all we could lay to rest the notion that it is a virtue to love others and a vice to love one-self. For what is vicious is not self-love but selfishness, and selfishness is more a product of self-hate, than self-love. All forms of selfishness are finally forms of insecurity, compensations for lack of self-love.

—— ❦ ——

Fear destroys intimacy. It distances us from each other; or makes us cling to each other, which is the death of freedom. Fear has so many ways to destroy life. Love alone can hold onto and recreate life. Only love can create intimacy, and freedom too, for when all hearts are one, nothing else has to be one—neither clothes nor age; neither sex nor sexual preference; race nor mind-set.

—— ❦ ——

If we hate ourselves, we can never love others, for love is the gift of oneself. How will you make a gift of that which you hate?

—— ❦ ——

I have always liked the old fairy tales in which the one who has turned into a beast can only regain human form through someone else's love. Here I think is the clue to love. Love is to make us more human, and that demands that we care so much for each other that we have not to be nice but to be honest. We *have* to be honest, for most real faults are hidden and therefore demand an outside revealer.

—— ❦ ——

I believe God dwells with those who make love their aim. And there is no sentimentality in this love; it is not endlessly pliable, always yielding. Prophets from Amos and Isaiah to Gandhi and King have shown how frequently compassion demands confrontation. Love without criticism is a kind of betrayal. Lying is done with silence as well as with words. And always the love that is of God lies on the far side of justice, never on the near side.

-------- ⟨≋⟩ --------

Rules at best are signposts, never hitching posts. Personally I doubt whether there is such a thing as a Christian rule. There are probably only acts that are more or less Christian depending on the motives prompting them. But if we say, "Down with rules," we must at the same time say, "Up with persons." And if we exalt freedom as Christians, we must remember that freedom is grounded in love. "He who does not love remains in death." Though setting no outer rules, love exacts much from within. As Paul Ramsay says, "If everything is permitted which Christian love permits, everything is demanded which Christian love requires." So let others say, "Anything goes." The Christian asks, "What does love require?"

In short, we have come up with love as an answer to legalism on the one hand and lawlessness on the other. Love hallows individuality. Love consecrates and never desecrates personality. Love demands that all our actions reflect a movement toward and not away from nor against each other. And love insists that all people assume their responsibility for all their relations.

-------- ⟨≋⟩ --------

Love is its own reward. For its inspiration, love does not depend on the pay it receives, which is why, out of hand, we have to reject all notions of heaven as pie in the sky by and by—deferred gratification. (I hate the way some TV evangelists try to overcome my self-ishness by appealing to my selfish motives!) But the fact of the matter is, love does have a reward. Just as the proper benefits of education are the opportunities of continuing education, so the rewards of loving are to become yet more vulnerable, more tender, more caring.

No sermon on love can fail to mention love's most difficult problem in our time— how to find effective ways to alleviate the massive suffering of humanity at home and abroad. What we need to realize is that to love effectively we must act collectively, and that in collective action personal relationships cannot ignore power relationships. Until Christians learn this truth of a technological, complex world, we shall be in this world as lap dogs trying to keep up with the wolf pack.

To show compassion for an individual without showing concern for the structures of society that make him an object of compassion is to be sentimental rather than loving.

To love is surely to support and to encourage—but not necessarily to approve. Quite the contrary! If we love one another we will help one another fight against our evil dreams. When through despair or self-pity we become dead to rapture, friends are needed to remind us that God made the rift of dawn, the reddening rose, Plato, and the Pleiades, to give us solace when life becomes rough. A friend is not one who puts her friendship before her friend, but rather one who risks her friendship for the sake of her friend.

Love measures our stature: the more we love, the bigger we are. There is no smaller package in all the world than that of a man all wrapped up in himself!

"He who loves father and mother more than me is not worthy of me." That's not really cruel. Loving Christ more than our fathers and mothers simply saves the love we have for our parents from idolatry. You remember the poem of Lovelace that goes

> I could not love thee, dear, so much,
> Loved I not honor more.
> (Richard Lovelace, "To Lucasta, Going to the Wars")

Substitute "Jesus" for "honor" and you have the formula for saving God-given mercies—our loved ones—from becoming a Satanic temptation: to think there's nothing more. I don't hear Christ asking us to pull the house down on the heads of our mothers and fathers, husbands, wives, and children. I hear him only reminding us that God, as the source of love, is the proper head of every loving household.

Love, and you are a success whether or not the world thinks so. The highest purpose of Christianity—which is primarily a way of ⌐ life, not a system of belief—is to love one another. And the first fruit of love is joy, the joy that represents meaning and fulfillment.

———— ⤳ ————

Too many religious people make faith their aim. They think "the greatest of these" is faith, and faith defined as all but infallible doctrine. These are the dogmatic, divisive Christians, more concerned with freezing the doctrine than warming the heart. If faith can be exclusive, love can only be inclusive.

———— ⤳ ————

It is clear that the greatest evils of humanity are due to lack of love and that the New Testament's "miraculous catch" (see Luke 5) was not the haddock and shad and whatever else Peter and the rest of them caught that day, but the fact that Peter and the rest were caught up, even as we are, in the net of Christ's love.

———— ⤳ ————

Many of us overvalue autonomy, the strength to stand alone, the capacity to act independently. Far too few of us pay attention to the virtues of dependence and interdependence, and especially to the capacity to be vulnerable. Learning, and especially unlearning, can take place only in the absence of defensiveness. When we drop our defenses, we can learn. And we can drop our defenses only when we love and are loved.

⁓

The world, of course, is in a frightful mess, but because of us, not because of God. God could only clean up the mess by taking away our freedom. But without freedom where could love be? So paradoxically, it is because God is a loving God that there is so much suffering in the world. But because God is a loving God he is suffering too, and suffering also through the bodies and souls of his creatures, which is why Paul writes, "For while we live we are always being given up to death for Jesus' sake."

⁓

Fixation, as ever, is blinding. Love, by contrast, is visionary, calling not only for obedience but also for the utmost in clear-sightedness. Faith is no substitute for thought; it's what makes good thinking possible.

⁓

Tolerance and passivity are a deadly combination. Together they allow us to tolerate the intolerable, to ignore the power of anger in works of love; for if you lessen your anger at the structures of power, you lower your love for the victims of power.

———— ❧ ————

Too often the churches have taught that the opposite of love is hate, just as they have taught that the opposite of peace is conflict. What the opposite of peace is I am not sure. I know it is not conflict, maybe not even violence; perhaps it is injustice. But as regards love, I am sure the Bible is right: the opposite of love is not hate but fear. "There is no fear in love, but perfect love casts out fear."

———— ❧ ————

If, as Scripture says, "God is love," then human freedom is real. As Dostoyevsky's Grand Inquisitor properly discerned, freedom is a burden, choice is scary. But freedom is the absolutely necessary precondition of love. We are not slaves but children of our Father, free to do good, free to sin. So when in anguish over any human violence done to innocent victims, we ask of God, "How could you let that happen?" it's well to remember that God at that very moment is asking the exact same question of us.

———— ❧ ————

"God is love," as Scripture says, and that means the revelation is in the relationship. "God is love" means God is known devotionally, not dogmatically. "God is love" does not clear up old mysteries; it discloses new mystery. "God is love" is not a truth we can master; it is only one to which we can surrender. Faith is being grasped by the power of love.

Not only Peter but all the apostles after Jesus' death were ten times the people they were before; that's irrefutable. It was in response to their enthusiasm (the word means "in God") that the opposition organized; and it was in response to the opposition—so many scholars believe—that the doctrine of the empty tomb arose, not as a cause but as a consequence of the Easter faith. The last chapter of Matthew may be literally true—I don't want to dispute it—but I also don't want any of you to stumble forever over it. Like many a miracle story in the Bible, it may be an expression of faith rather than a basis of faith.

Convinced by his appearances that Jesus was their living Lord, the disciples really had only one category in which to articulate this conviction, and that was the doctrine of the resurrection of the dead. To St. Paul, the events of the last days had been anticipated, and God, by a mighty act, had raised Jesus from the dead—in a spiritual body. In Paul's writings, the living Christ and the Holy Spirit are never clearly differentiated, so that when he says, "Not I, but Christ who dwells within me," he is talking about the same Holy Spirit that you and I can experience in our own lives. I myself believe passionately in the resurrection of Jesus Christ, because in my own life I have experienced Christ not as a memory, but as a presence. So today on Easter we gather not, as it were, to close the show with the tune "Thanks for the Memory," but rather to reopen the show with the hymn "Jesus Christ Is Risen Today."

Social Justice and Civil Liberties

There is no longer Jew or Greek,
there is no longer slave or free,
there is no longer male and female;
for all of you are one in Christ Jesus.
                              —Galatians 3:28

In Christ there is no East or West
In Him no South or North;
But one great fellowship of love
Throughout the whole wide earth.
                              —John Oxenham

Freedom will not come
Today, this year
Nor ever
Through compromise and fear. . . .
Freedom
Is a strong seed
planted
in a great need.
I live here too;
I want freedom
Just as you.
    —Langston Hughes, "Freedom"

*A*m I my brother's keeper?" No, I am my brother's brother or sister. Human unity is not something we are called upon to create, only to recognize.

We all belong one to another. That's the way God made us. Christ died to keep us that way. Our sin is only and always that we put asunder what God has joined together.

Prejudice disfigures the observer, not the person observed. If only the latter could remember it.

"To be more safe the nations at length become willing to run the risk of being less free." So wrote Alexander Hamilton. We may become more concerned with defense than in having things worth defending.

———

Trent Lott, Gary Bauer, Pat Robertson, Jerry Falwell—all insist their words contribute nothing to an atmosphere that might legitimate anti-gay violence. Don't they know that the seed of disrespect often blossoms into hatred and violence?

———

Diversity may be both the hardest thing to live with and the most dangerous thing to be without.

———

This isn't a matter of charity, but of justice. Just as to the slaves freedom was not a gift but the restoration of a right no one had any business taking from them, so a home is a right; the homeless are being robbed.

———

There are people and things in this world, and people are to be loved and things are to be used. And it is increasingly important that we love people and use things, for there is so much in our gadget-minded, consumer-oriented society that is encouraging us to love things and use people.

------ ≋ ------

Truth is always in danger of being sacrificed on the altars of good taste and social stability.

------ ≋ ------

The final end of life lies not in politics, but the final end of life is concerned with the proper ordering of power to the end that it may enhance and not destroy human life. Only a fool hasn't learned in the twentieth century that the political order in which people live deeply affects the personal lives they lead.

------ ≋ ------

Law is not as disinterested as our concepts of law pretend; law serves power; law in large measure is a recapitulation of the status quo; it confirms a rigid order designed to insulate the beneficiaries of the status quo from the disturbances of change. The painful truth—one with a long history—is that police are around in large part to guarantee a peaceful digestion for the rich.

------ ≋ ------

In the long run, as Gamaliel seemed to recognize, what stands between man and chaos is not laws but good laws. The Civil Rights Law of 1964 stands between man and chaos, but did the Fugitive Slave Act?

It is important to keep recalling that racial justice and gender equality are morally and constitutionally "center." To call those promoting them "leftist" is dishonest, something usually done by rightwing politicians who appeal to the political center by attacking the moral center.

A feminist is basically someone who refuses to be a masochist.

The woman most in need of liberation is the woman in every man.

To their credit, college admissions people have become far more intentional in recruiting minorities. You *have* to seek out people to whom life appears a game that often is rigged against them. This special recruitment is beneficial to everyone because our lives are rife with misconceptions of each other *and of ourselves*. Universities should be communities to rescue us from bias and self-deception, and the two are interrelated. To quote James Baldwin, "If I am not what you say I am, then you are not who you think you are."

———— ⊂≋⊃ ————

Another pseudo fact that we need to dethrone is that the economic and social problems of the country are largely due today to giving minorities an even chance. This belief is spectacularly out of touch. The 800,000 farms lost in the 1980s weren't lost to blacks (who themselves lost thousands of farms); the thousands of manufacturing jobs lost didn't go to blacks. In fact, an estimated two million jobs in the '80s left the country in pursuit of low wages and high profits.

———— ⊂≋⊃ ————

Scapegoating always arises when, instead of facing real wrongs, people are maddened with imaginary ones. It often appears that the more harm we white Americans do to black Americans, the more harm we claim they have done to us. We grab everything for ourselves, even the injuries!

———— ⊂≋⊃ ————

When will we men get over the notion—largely unconscious—that our lives are somehow more important than those of women, even of women we love?

— ⟨⟩ —

How easy always for the victors to "sound fine words unsoundly." Think how the rich and powerful in this country, having initiated practically nothing in civil rights, loudly insisted on "responsible Negro leadership," completely begging the question—responsive to what, white interests or Black needs?

— ⟨⟩ —

However complicated it may be to implement, there is a need for affirmative action. It is prompted by years of negative action. Without affirmative action, the first steps toward admitting African Americans would never have been taken. "Equal opportunity" only reflects good intentions; affirmative action registers results.

— ⟨⟩ —

A nation that puts so much stress on getting ahead has a hard time dealing with those who fall behind. If you're successful, you seldom identify with failure. This is proved by the fact that integration of races has already resulted in an even greater segregation by class. The so-called underclass has all the markings of a subordinate caste. In the long run, I believe, class will prove a tougher nut to crack than race.

— ⟨⟩ —

It is not Scripture that creates hostility to homosexuality, but rather hostility to homosexuals that prompts some Christians to recite a few sentences from Paul and retain passages from an otherwise discarded Old Testament law code. In abolishing slavery and in ordaining women we've gone beyond biblical literalism. It's time we did the same with gays and lesbians. The problem is not how to reconcile homosexuality with scriptural passages that condemn it, but rather how to reconcile the rejection and punishment of homosexuals with the love of Christ. It can't be done. So instead of harping on what's "natural," let's talk of what's "normal," what operates according to the norm. For Christians the norm is Christ's love. If people can show the tenderness and constancy in caring that honors Christ's love, what matters their sexual orientation? Shouldn't a relationship be judged by its inner worth rather than by its outer appearance? When has a monopoly on durable life-warming love been held by legally wed heterosexuals?

----- ⟡ -----

So enough of these fixed certainties. If what we think is right and wrong divides still further the human family, there must be something wrong with what we think is right. Enough of this cruelty and hatred, this punitive legislation toward gay people. Peter widened his horizons; let's not narrow ours. It has been said that a mind once stretched by a new idea can never return to its former shape. Let's listen, let's learn, let's read and pray—none of this is easy—until with Peter's conviction we can make a similar confession: "Truly I perceive that God shows no partiality, but in every sexual orientation anyone who fears him and does what is right is acceptable to him."

----- ⟡ -----

It's time to realize that any belief in biblical inerrancy is itself unbiblical. Read the story of Peter and Cornelius (Acts 10) and you will see that scriptural writings do not support the inerrancy of Scripture. Besides, Christians believe in the Word made flesh, not the Word made words. Christianity is less a set of beliefs than a way of life, and a way of life that actually warns against absolute intellectual certainty: "O the depth of the riches both of the wisdom and knowledge of God! How unsearchable are God's judgments and God's ways past finding out! For who has known the mind of God?" (Rom. 11:33–34).

I think we know far more of God's heart than we do of the mind of God.

It's God's heart that Christ on the cross lays bare for the whole world to see. And "God is love, and those who abide in love abide in God, and God abides in them" (1 John 4:16)—that passage suggests that revelation is in the relationship. And a relationship with God provides more psychological certitude than intellectual certainty. Faith is not believing without proof; it is trusting without reservation. I think all belief systems that rest on absolute intellectual certainty—be that certainty the doctrine of papal infallibility or the doctrine of the verbal inerrancy of Scripture—all such belief systems should go out the stained glass windows, for they have no proper place in church. They induce Christians to sharpen their minds by narrowing them. They make Christians doctrinaire, dogmatic, mindlessly militant. To such absolute belief systems can be attributed all manner of unchristian horrors such as inquisitions and holy wars, witch burning, morbid guilt, unthinking conformity, self-righteousness, anti-Semitism, misogyny, and homophobia.

The argument that gays threaten to destroy heterosexual marriage is an assertion only, not an argument. If anyone destroys marriage, it's married people, not gays.

––––– ⟨≋⟩ –––––

People who say "same-sex marriage makes me uncomfortable" should probably remind themselves that comfort has nothing to do with the issue and that, often as not, change is discomforting. I think those of us who are straight people really need to sit down quietly and compare our own discomfort with the discomfort of gays and lesbians who for years have been excluded, isolated, silenced, abused, and even killed.

––––– ⟨≋⟩ –––––

As a man I consider myself at best a recovering chauvinist. As a white person I am a recovering racist, and as a straight person a recovering heterosexist. To women, African Americans, gays and lesbians, I am deeply grateful for stretching my mind, deepening my heart, and convincing me that no human being should ever be patient with prejudice at the expense of its victims.

––––– ⟨≋⟩ –––––

In 1896 in Plessy v. Ferguson, the United States Supreme Court found "separate but equal" to be constitutional in educating black and white children. Would not the same inequality prove true were civil marriage reserved for straight couples only while gay and lesbian unions were designated otherwise? Further, if for all of us marriage is a profound symbol, and for some a sacred one, what right have straight people to deny it to gays and lesbians for whom it is altogether as meaningful?

I can't even remember the name of the student who in April of 1961 late at night in a kitchen in North Carolina told me his story of a sit-in at a Greensboro lunch counter: "The five of us came in and sat down on what empty stools there were. Pretty soon the man behind the counter slipped out. In the mirror I could see the crowd begin to gather on the sidewalk outside. Then the other folks on the stools began to go out whether they had finished or not, and without paying, seeing there was no one left to pay. The five of us moved together for a little warmth. Then in the mirror I was relieved to see the police. But no sooner had they appeared than they disappeared, deliberately. That was the signal. The crowd began to come in. You could just smell their anger. Some of them began to shout insults into one of my ears while from the other side a guy starts to blow cigarette smoke into my eyes. I'm gripping the counter. Then the guy with the cigarette puts it out on the back of my hand. I think I'm going to faint. Then I feel a knee in the middle of my back, then an arm around my neck. Someone is pulling my hair, hard. Pretty soon I'm on the floor, trying to stay curled up in a ball. They were really kicking us. When we were practically unconscious, the police reappeared and arrested all five of us lying on the floor for disturbing the peace. In jail they roughed us up some more, just for good measure. Then came the best part. When I got out I called home and my mother told me, 'Good Negroes don't go to jail.'"

I can't remember this student's name, but he made it easy for me to go on a freedom ride the following month.

Martin Luther King deserves a national holiday because he rescued the American people from the shallows and miseries where they had chosen to live their lives. He deserves a national holiday because more than any other public figure in this century he asserted his individuality in order to affirm community on the widest possible scale; because better than any other public figure he understood the nature of compassion, that it did not exclude confrontation. It was Martin's message that it is not enough to suffer with the poor; we must confront the people and systems that cause poverty. It was Martin's message that you cannot set the captive free if you are not willing to confront those who hold the keys. Without confrontation compassion becomes merely commiseration, fruitless and sentimental.

Likewise King understood the difference between defiance and freedom. Confrontation to him did not mean the ruin and humiliation of opponents. Nonviolence to him represented conquest without the humiliation of the conquered. Nonviolence to him represented an effort to give visibility not to our own poor powers but to God's everlasting love. "Not unto us, O Lord, not unto us, but unto thy name be the glory." Nonviolence represented a chance for all parties to rise above their present condition.

Measured by feet, it was a short distance from King's pulpit to the streets of Montgomery. Measured spiritually, it was a long journey. But he took it, in the name of him who "in those days . . . came from Nazareth to Galilee and was baptized by John in the Jordan."

"We hold these truths to be self-evident, that all men are created equal, that they are endowed by their Creator with certain unalienable rights."

Let me suggest that for over two hundred years the great social struggles of America have aimed to make the Constitution more consonant with the Declaration of Independence. Counting the first ten, the Bill of Rights, the Constitution now has twenty-six amendments. The eleventh, passed in 1795, is about federal judicial jurisdiction; two are about Prohibition and its repeal; three others deal with the presidency—election, limitation, and succession. The other twenty—every one, whether it be granting freedom to slaves or votes to women, outlawing the poll tax or instituting the income tax, lowering the voting age or giving residents of D.C. the right to vote for the president—every one mandates an extension of democracy.

I believe one significant cure for what presently ails us lies in extending yet further our democracy. We need more women's rights, not less, until they are genuinely equal to men's rights. We need more gay rights, more rights for immigrants, for children, for the more than one million of our citizens in jail. We need to recognize that affirmative action is good for all of us, as the ex-presidents of Harvard and Princeton have recently reported. And given the vast wealth and power that have accumulated in the hands of a small and self-serving corporate elite, which pays itself proportionately more and pays workers proportionately less than in any other industrialized democracy, we need to democratize the market economy of America. I can still remember from high school days—it was in 1939—hearing Franklin Roosevelt say, "My fellow Americans, progress is not measured by how much we add to the abundance of those who already have a great deal, but rather by how much we do for those who have too little."

Social Justice and Economic Rights

And what does the LORD require of you
but to do justice, and to love kindness,
and to walk humbly with your God?
　　　　　　　—Micah 6:8

The LORD enters into judgment
　　with the elders and princes of his people:
It is you who have devoured the vineyard,
　　the spoil of the poor is in your houses.
What do you mean by crushing my people
　　by grinding the face of the poor? says the Lord GOD of hosts.
　　　　　　　—Isaiah 3:14

Lest our feet stray from the places,
our God where we met thee,
Lest our hearts drunk with the wine of
the world, we forget thee.
Shadowed beneath thy hand
May we forever stand
True to our God, true to our native land.
　　　　　　　—James Weldon Johnson

We can have a democracy or we can have great wealth concentrated in the hands of the few. We cannot have both.
　　　　　　　—Justice Louis Brandeis

47

I believe Christianity is a worldview that undergirds progressive thought and action. I believe the church doesn't so much have a social ethic as it is a social ethic.

—— ⌘ ——

Public good doesn't automatically follow from private virtue. A person's moral character, sterling though it may be, is insufficient to serve the cause of justice, which is to challenge the status quo, to try to make what's legal more moral, to speak truth to power, and to take personal or concerted action against evil, whether in personal or systemic form.

(John D. Rockefeller!)

—— ⌘ ——

Not to take sides is effectively to weigh in on the side of the stronger.

------ ⊗ ------

We say we're tough on crime; we're only tough on criminals. Were we tough on crime we'd put the money up front, in prevention, in building communities, not more prisons. We forget that crime is a moral as well as a legal problem. Some of us are guilty but all of us are responsible. We stress the guilty to exonerate the others also responsible for a soaring crime rate.

------ ⊗ ------

Ninety-eight percent of people in prison in the United States lived in poverty most of their lives. Nearly 1 of every 150 people in this country is imprisoned, a number no other democracy comes close to matching.

------ ⊗ ------

The Bible is less concerned with alleviating the effects of injustice than in eliminating the causes of it.

------ ⊗ ------

To know God is to do justice. To recognize this implacable moral imperative of the faith represents the kind of good religion that mixes well with politics.

------ ≋ ------

When we are intent on being, rather than on having, we are happier. And when we are intent on being, we don't take away from other people's being—in fact, we enhance it. But when we are intent on having, we create have-nots—and invariably lie about the connection.

------ ≋ ------

To believe you can approach transcendence without drawing nearer in compassion to suffering humanity is to fool yourself. There can be no genuine personal religious conversion without a change in social attitude.

------ ≋ ------

Compassion and justice are companions, not choices.

------ ≋ ------

It is ironic to think of the number of people in this country who pray for the poor and needy on Sunday and spend the rest of the week complaining that the government is doing something about them.

------- ⊂⊃ -------

"Unto us a child is born." The same risk Abraham took in going out into the world, God took—and more—coming into it. So what shall we say this Advent: a risk for a risk, a birth for us, a rebirth for God? But let us be clear: the point of a rebirth is not to stay young, but to grow up. The point of a rebirth is to claim, as did Abraham, his God-given freedom: the freedom, at last, to rise above the moral squalor of prevailing opportunism; at last, no longer to render everything to Caesar; at last, no longer to acquiesce passively in evil (an acquiescence we often dignify in private life with the word "patience," and in public life with the word "patriotism.") But passive acquiescence in evil represents only one thing: the sin of cowardice.

------- ⊂⊃ -------

"Power tends to corrupt; and absolute power corrupts absolutely" (Lord Acton). That is true. But failure to assume responsibility for power is also corrupting and devastating today in its effects. For evil is not so much the work of a few degenerate people or groups of people as it is the result of the indifference and negligence of the many.

------- ⊂⊃ -------

With spiritual arrogance goes the itch to destroy. History warns that the best is always a hair's breadth from the worst, and that heartless moralists in the corridors of power are those who start inquisitions.

———— ❧ ————

Hell is truth seen too late.

———— ❧ ————

Jesus never said bread wasn't important—"Give us this day our daily bread"—and, in fact, he did everything he could to feed the poor. With Mary, his mother, he believed that God "has filled the hungry with good things, and the rich he has sent empty away." How angry he must be with the way our government is now filling the rich with good things, and sending the poor empty away. How he would scorn an economic theory that says we must heap more on the platters of the rich, for only so will more crumbs fall to the poor. Never has a government climbed off the backs of the upper class so fast to tap-dance on the backs of the poor. Never in recent history have we had so blatant a plutocracy: a government of the wealthy, by the wealthy, and for the wealthy.

———— ❧ ————

When the rich take from the poor, it's called an economic plan. When the poor take from the rich, it's called class warfare. It must be wonderful for President Bush to deplore class warfare while making sure his class wins.

-------- ⬡ --------

Not only Christians but all Americans subscribe to the notion that "all people are created equal." But how many *feel* the monstrosity of inequality? I'm thinking not only of racial inequality, but also of today's excess of wealth and poverty, the absence of affordable housing that "Mr. Conservative," Senator Robert Taft, in the 1940s considered a moral imperative. (The stated goal of the 1948 Taft Housing Legislation was a decent home for every American family.) Few of us today are troubled by the way our economy flourishes not by providing necessities but by providing luxuries, and by the national goal of ending welfare as we know it, when a more just goal would be seeking to end poverty as we know it. We Christians mean well—feebly. We may be repelled by materialism, but we are caught up in it. We are troubled by widespread poverty, but we overly esteem wealth. In short, ours generally is a superficial religious identity, and a superficial religious identity is just that—superficial.

-------- ⬡ --------

The word "homeless" is devastating, suggesting neither comfort nor companionship, dignity nor grace, and precious little identity. To have no place is to be no place. Homelessness is nowheresville—

whether you're one of the world's 14 million refugees, a boat person from Indochina, one of Calcutta's 400,000 semi-starved sidewalk dwellers, or one of the 36,000 who in New York City spend so much of their time huddled in doorways, wrapping themselves in the *Daily News.*

----- ≈≈≈ -----

"Those who oppress the poor insult their Maker" (Prov. 14:31). But the hard question is, how are the poor to be helped—by charity or by justice, by voluntary contribution or by legislation? In the book of Acts we read of the first Christian communities: "There was not a needy person among them, for as many as were possessors of lands or houses sold them . . . and distribution was made to each as any had need" (Acts 2:44–45). It was all voluntary. But those were small communities, charismatic, filled with the Holy Spirit, visited regularly by one apostle or another; their people were poor and far removed from the corrupting seats of power. Should we hold them up as models for churches? Yes, by all means. Should we hold them up as a model for society at large? Alas, no.

Human nature is sinful, and therefore the virtue of the few will never compensate for the inertia of the many. Rich people and rich nations will not voluntarily open their eyes to see the biblical truth that the poor have ownership rights in their surplus. This they will see only in retrospect, after their surplus is taken away—by legislation, hopefully, not by violence. Given human goodness, voluntary contributions are possible, but given human sinfulness, legislation is indispensable. Charity, yes always; but never as a substitute for justice. What we keep forgetting in this country is that people have rights, basic rights: the right to food, the right to decent housing, the right to medical care, the right to education. Food pantries like the one we have here at Riverside, and shelters for the homeless throughout the city, are painful reminders of how the richest country in the world still denies fundamental human rights to the poorest of its citizens.

———

We cannot legislate morality, only the conditions conducive to morality. Martin Luther King used to say, "You can't make them love us, but you can stop them from lynching us." Likewise, we can't force people to love the poor, but we ought to be able to stop starving them to death—some 500 million of them around the world. We ought to be able to see that just as the Sabbath belongs to man so the economy belongs to human beings, not human beings to the economy. Economics are not a science; they are only politics in disguise. It grieves me that we in this nation of abundance passively heed economists who assure us that full employment is impossible, that social welfare programs are too inflationary, that taxing wealth will result in "failure to provide sufficient replacement to maintain capital intact." These same economists rarely mention the following statistic: had the world spent for the poor one million dollars every day since the birth of Jesus Christ, it would have spent but one-half of what the Reagan administration wants to spend in five years on the U.S. military alone—1.5 trillion dollars.

———

Of course we are to feed the poor, just as did Jesus. In the phrase "Man does not live by bread alone," the important word is not "bread," but "alone." Human rights hardly exhaust the gospel, but they are at the heart of it, not ancillary to it.

———— ⁂ ————

The biblical reminder is clear: whatever our economic system, the enemy is excess, not possessions. The battle cry is "Enough!" not "Nothing!" "Enough" so that we can all break bread together, so that everyone's prayer can be answered—"Give us this day our daily bread."

———— ⁂ ————

There are two ways to be rich: one is to have a lot of money; the other is to have few needs. Let us remember that Jesus—who influenced history more than any other single person, institution, or nation—died, his sole possession a robe.

———— ⁂ ————

What business have we reversing the priorities of Mary's *Magnificat*, filling the rich with good things and sending the poor empty away? There's nothing in any sacred scripture anywhere that says that the whims of the rich should best the rights of the poor. How, Sunday by Sunday, can Christians pray, "Forgive us our debts" and not think of Third World countries, some of whom are spending three to five times as much paying off foreign debt as they do on basic services to their own people?

In the United States grim poverty is a tragedy that great wealth makes a sin.

"He who is kind to the poor lends to the Lord." Isn't that a wonderful thought? If we voluntarily give of our surplus, and if we fight for justice, we are helping the poor, yes, but more than that: we are helping the Creator of heaven and earth; we are helping God with a loan! "He who is kind to the poor *lends* to the Lord." And I leave it to your experience and imagination to surmise what the repayment of that loan might be, for "eye has not seen, nor ear heard, neither have entered into the heart of man, the things which God hath prepared for them that love him."

Ponder the fact that all those conspicuously "called" in the Bible—like Moses—were called through the voices, the sorrows of the poor. All the prophets responded to the voices of the oppressed. Think then of what we receive when we accept the invitation to become Good Samaritans. We receive our identity; we receive our life. Once again "we pass out of death into life because we love the brothers and sisters." Yes, indeed, as Saint Francis said, "It is in giving that we receive."

Believers know that while our values are embodied in tradition, our hopes are always located in change.

It's the noneconomic uses of money that make money so complicated, even demonic. Jesus saw the demonic side when he saw money as a rival god capable of inspiring great devotion: "You cannot serve God and mammon." Note that only money is put on a par with God, not knowledge, not family nobility, not reputation, not talent: only money is elevated to divine status. No wonder Jesus talked more about money than any other subject except the kingdom of God.

Today we Americans are not marching in the ways of the Lord but limping along in our own ways, thinking not of the public weal but of our private interests. Today tax cutting is more popular than social spending, even for the poorest Americans. And because we have so cruelly separated freedom from virtue—because we define freedom in a morally inferior way—our "union strong and great" is stalled in a storm.

It is not money that poisons the soul; it is being anxious about it.

When "enrich thyself" is the prevailing ethos, common integrity is made to look like courage. In the words of a le Carré character, "You have to think like a hero to behave like a decent human being." And the irony is that the young bent upon becoming wealthy and thinking they are fulfilling themselves are in fact limiting themselves.

One of the attributes of power is that it gives those who have it the ability to define reality and the power to make others believe in their definition. Thus it is that private property in America has come to be considered all but sacred. Obviously this makes its redistribution difficult, even through taxation.

I have nothing but appreciation for the freedom offered faculty and students to think and say pretty much what they please. But that freedom is vastly exalted over any obligation to do any good to anyone. This is so because inevitably every country's education reflects that country's ideology. When the prevailing ethos is "enrich thyself," the humanities tend to become but cultural icing on an economic cake.

The way we are cutting taxes for the wealthy and social programs for the poor, you'd think the greedy were needy and the needy were greedy.

———— ❧ ————

The primary problems of the planet arise not from the poor, for whom education is the answer; they arise from the well-educated, for whom self-interest is the problem.

———— ❧ ————

Christ is not only a healer of individuals. He is also a prophet to the nations. While he walked the earth, Jesus delivered people from paralysis, insanity, leprosy, suppurating wounds, deformity, and muteness. But again and again in word and deed he returned to the plight of the poor, whose poverty, in true prophetic fashion, he considered no historical accident, but the fruit of social injustice. What would he say and do in our hard and uncertain times, in a world of thirteen million refugees, a world one-half of whose children never so much as open their mouths to say "aah" to a doctor, a world in which almost every country is robbing the poor to feed the military? And would he not pronounce our own nation a greedy disgrace? Whole cities could live on the garbage from our dumps, on the luxuries we consider necessities. The world with its triumphs and despairs, its beauty and ugliness, has today moved next door to every one of us. Only spiritual deafness can prevent our hearing the voice of God in the clamor of the cities. Only blindness of a willful sort can prevent our seeing the face of the Risen Lord in the faces of the suffering poor. The glory of God is the human race fully alive, and that means at least minimally fed, clothed, and housed.

So let us indeed not delude ourselves: you cannot have a revolt without revolting conditions. Communism has never come to a nation that took care of its poor, its aged, its youth, its sick, and its handicapped.

Isaiah understood what Lord Acton failed to note, that it is not only power that tends to corrupt, and absolute power absolutely; powerlessness does the same. It produces lives dreary with self-hatred and stingy with hope.

Had I but one wish for the churches of America I think it would be that they come to see the difference between charity and justice. Charity is a matter of personal attributes; justice, a matter of public policy. Charity seeks to alleviate the effects of injustice; justice seeks to eliminate the causes of it. Charity in no way affects the status quo, while justice leads inevitably to political confrontation. Especially I would hope that Christians would see that the compassion that moved the Good Samaritan to act charitably—that same compassion prompted biblical prophets to confront injustice, to speak truth to power, as did Jesus, who, though more than a prophet, was certainly nothing less.

------ ⊗ ------

"And what does the Lord require of you but to do justice. . . ." "Justice is to sort out what belongs to whom, and to return it to them." (Brueggemann). Justice then redescribes the world. And to do justice as God does justice is to intervene in the social order as did Moses in Pharaoh's court when he insisted on freedom for the Hebrew slaves; as did Nathan in David's court when he protested the king's rapacious action against Uriah the Hittite; as did Elijah when he thundered against Ahab and Jezebel for having done in Naboth in order to take his land.

------ ⊗ ------

Asked to comment on Jesus' saying "Render unto Caesar the things which are Caesar's and unto God the things which are God's," Dorothy Day took a moment or two to think and then replied, "If we were to render unto God all the things which are God's, there would be nothing left for Caesar."

------ ⊗ ------

While Christianity does not give specific answers to specific social problems, it does shed light on these problems, and we all must try as best we can to carry our Christian insights out into the streets and byways of life.

What Christians in particular must remember is that moral outrage is a wonderful motivator but no formula for a solution.

Honesty does not come painlessly: "The truth will make you free" (St. Paul), but first it makes you miserable! That God is against the status quo is one of the hardest things to believe if you are a Christian who happens to profit by the status quo. In fact, most of us don't really believe it, not in our heart of hearts. We comfort ourselves with the thought that because our intentions are good (nobody gets up in the morning and says, "Whom can I oppress today?"), we do not have to examine the consequences of our actions. As a matter of fact, many of us are even eager to respond to injustice, as long as we can do so without having to confront the causes of it. And there's the great pitfall of charity. Handouts to needy individuals are genuine, necessary responses to injustice, but they do not necessarily face the reason for the injustice. And that is why President Reagan and so many business leaders today are promoting charity: it is desperately needed in an economy whose prosperity is based on growing inequality. First these leaders proclaim themselves experts on matters economic, and prove it by taking the most out of the economy! Then they promote charity as if it were the work of the church, finally telling us troubled clergy to shut up and bless the economy as once we blessed the battleships.

---- ⊰⊱ ----

The prophet did not say, "Let charity roll down like mighty waters"—because giving without receiving is a downward motion. The prophet said, "Let *justice* roll down like mighty waters, and righteousness like an ever-flowing stream." Therefore, for all his eloquence, the Pope was wrong only to flay the rich; he should have followed the lead of liberation theologians and told the poor to organize. For that apparently is the way God intervenes in history. The exodus story tells us that liberation is primarily the work of the oppressed themselves.

---- ⊰⊱ ----

I believe the herd mentality dominates us today, and for this reason: we have allowed agreement to become the basis of our unity instead of mutual concern. And when agreement instead of mutual concern becomes the basis of unity, when we start agreeing our way through life, then crucifixions take place. For then "Play it safe," "Don't rock the boat," become the Commandment on which are "hanged" all the law and the prophets. For it is the Commandment that drops a mask of dissimulation over the face of truth, the Commandment that makes us turn our backs on screams in the night, that makes us turn the other cheek in order not to see the evil, that makes us hide behind our specialties, claiming lack of knowledge of the things that make us collaborators with the very forces of evil we condemn. Now we too kill. For what else is our apathetic avoidance of politics today than a sophisticated version of unsophisticated Cain clubbing his brother to death?

Perhaps the crucial question is this: Is charity ever a substitute for justice? I've listened to many a Marxist accuse the churches of having a vested interest in unjust structures that produce victims to whom good Christians can then pour out their hearts in charity. I've listened and I've shuddered, because so often in history it's been so true. In other words, if there is a danger in politicizing the faith—a danger we are coming to—there is also a counterdanger, which is depoliticizing the faith. In times of oppression, if you don't translate choices of faith into political choices, you run the danger of washing your hands, like Pilate, and thereby, like Pilate, plaiting anew Christ's crown of thorns for "in as much as ye did it unto the least of these my brethren, ye did it unto me." In Scripture, there is no purely spiritual answer to slavery; no purely spiritual answer to the pain of the poor, nor to the arrogance of tyrants. In Scripture charity is no substitute for justice, anymore than is ritual, no matter how beautiful. "Take away from me the noise of your songs; to the melody of your hearts, I will not listen. But let justice roll down like mighty waters, and righteousness like an ever-flowing stream."

How are we to contrast Jesus' vision of things and the people's expectations? Are we to say he was a spiritual Messiah as opposed to a political one? Heaven forbid! That's the great Palm Sunday "cop-out" that will be proclaimed from pulpits all over the land today. Had Jesus been as nonpolitical as these pulpiteers, you can be sure the nails would never have grazed his palms. In the best prophetic tradition Jesus stood for the relief and protection of the poor and persecuted; for such use of the riches of creation that the world might be freed from famine, poverty, and disaster. And in the best prophetic tradition, he saw that the real troublemakers were not the ignorant and cruel, but the intelligent and corrupt. In contrast to so many of today's pulpiteers, Jesus knew that "Love your enemies" didn't mean "Don't make any!"

All our early American leaders had read Montesquieu, who differentiated despotism from monarchy from democracy. In each of these forms of society he found a governing principle: for despotism it was fear, for monarchy it was honor, and for democracy it was virtue. Because freedom was practically synonymous with virtue, we turned out a generation of politicians named Washington, Jefferson, Adams, Franklin, Hamilton.

Today with a population eighty times the three million who were Americans in 1776, we don't produce many leaders like that anymore, and the reason is clear; as Plato said, "What's honored in a country will be cultivated there." We have wonderful athletes and generally inferior politicians, and we deserve them both. Because we have so cruelly separated freedom from virtue, because we define freedom in a morally inferior way, we have entered what Herman Melville called the "Dark Ages of Democracy," a time when, as he predicted, the New Jerusalem would turn into Babylon, and Americans would experience what he called "the arrest of hope's advance."

There is a real temptation to think that an issue is less spiritual for being more political, to believe that religion is above politics, that the sanctuary is too sacred a place for the grit and grime of political battle. But if you believe religion is above politics, you are, in actuality, for the status quo—a very political position. And were God the god of the status quo, then the church would have no prophetic role, serving the state mainly as a kind of ambulance service.

Jesus was concerned most with those society counted least and put last. A politically engaged spirituality can never neglect the plight of those most deprived and vulnerable and will insist that improving the lot of the most oppressed is the decisive test of political sincerity. I believe in interreligious reverence, and believe further that a spiritual and ethical renewal of all the great religions of the world would be the greatest countervailing force to present-day economic interests that, in their pursuit of profits and growth, are so relentless as to make even governments more accountable to the market than to their own citizens.

In times of oppression, personal faith has to lead us to political choices; otherwise Christianity encourages fatalism on the part of the poor who, to keep themselves going, have only the promises of a better hereafter, and cynicism on the part of the rich, who feel they can do almost anything to the poor as long as they attend church and baptize their children.

The separation of Church and State is a sound doctrine, but it points to an organizational separation. It is not designed to separate Christians from their politics. For our faith certainly should inform our common life, as well as our personal, more private lives.

---⨳---

A politically committed spirituality contends against wrong without becoming wrongly contentious. It confronts national self-righteousness without personal self-righteousness. It cherishes God's creation; it serves the poor; it is not interested in the might of a nation but in the goodness of its people.

---⨳---

Truth is above harmony. Those who fear disorder more than injustice invariably produce more of both.

---⨳---

My dream for America is to see economic justice established in an atmosphere of democratic freedom. But I am old enough to have seen how corruption works in a democracy, how the taint of it spreads bit by bit, touching one person and then another, until it is

carried by a whole culture. I have seen how painfully and degrad-
ingly simple it is for leaders to deceive the people. Foreigners, for
example, are often struck at how many Americans, even poor Americans, think privilege is something earned or deserved. Rarely do
Americans see privilege as a form of theft.

Let me suggest that we not look overly to our political leaders. As
their ethical impulses tend to be so much weaker than their political
ones, in order not to stand out they'll do most anything to fit in.
They're right to think that politics is the art of the possible, but
wrong to forget that politics is also the art of making possible tomorrow what seems impossible today.

Already it is by the laws and policies of this country—whether we
are talking about an insane war abroad or the mental genocide that
takes place in slum schools—it is by the laws and policies of this
country that the consciences of people are being racked. Of course
we need to be concerned for order. Without it there is chaos, and
with chaos there is no justice. But today what Christians in particular need to remember is that God never stands for stability at the
expense of truth, that God has no interest in any status quo whatso-
ever. For God does not want to freeze history, but rather to move it
continually toward that ultimate goal of his kind of unity in justice
and mercy.

So what the Christian community needs to do above all else is to
raise up men and women of thought and of conscience, adventure-
some, imaginative people capable of both joy and suffering. And

most of all they must be people of courage so that when the day goes hard and cowards steal from the field, like Luther they will be able to say, "My conscience is captive to the word of God . . . to go against conscience is neither right nor safe. Here I stand. I can do no other. God help me."

———— ⚜ ————

Our faith should quell our fears, never our courage.

———— ⚜ ————

It is not that the weak are virtuous. No, as power corrupts the strong, so lack of it corrupts the weak. Suspicion, intolerance, apathy—all these fruits of weakness characterize life in the slums. But truth is a liability. It can be championed only at cost. Therefore the victors of society, with more to lose, always have more to gain by avoiding truth. Therefore Jesus could say, "It is easier for a camel to pass through the eye of a needle than for a rich man to enter the kingdom of heaven." And therefore we can say with a fair degree of accuracy that while the rich have given us our standards of taste it has generally been the poor who have told us what is right and wrong.

———— ⚜ ————

There can be no truth that passes over injustice in silence; nor can there be any moral virtue that condones it. The moral order may not exhaust the beauty of holiness, but it is an essential part of it, for in the grandeur of the prophets' vision the whole world swings on an ethical hinge. Mess with that hinge and history and even nature will feel the shock.

------- ⬦ -------

Too often we picture God as some immovable rock, when in fact it is God and God alone who never rests. I only quote Scripture: "He neither slumbers nor sleeps." It is God who says, "Behold, I create all things new." Therefore God's most persistent enemies must be those who are unwilling to move in new directions. . . . If you choose, you're sometimes wrong; but if you never choose, you're always wrong.

------- ⬦ -------

We Americans are today rightly suspicious of those in high office, for the events of recent years have shown us more than we have wanted to know about the arrogance of power. But we tend to forget the degree to which the inertia of the powerless makes possible the powerful. We tend to forget that in God's eyes self-obliteration is just as wicked as self-exaltation. Both stem from the same fateful error of confusing a person's talents with a person's value.

------- ⬦ -------

Paradoxically, now that we've become the most powerful nation in the world, we haven't the same positive influence we once had when, as a people, we were weakest. The American way of life is not the automatic choice of other people, as frequently it has been fashioned not to the enrichment but to the detriment of theirs. And at home the hammer of freedom is so frequently divorced from the chisel of justice that the common good, often as not, is identified with the good of those in power.

Globalization of the economy, it is claimed, will "lift all boats." Today it's becoming clear that it will "lift all yachts." It's not doing much for those on their leaking life rafts. Yet the economy inevitably will be more globalized, only hopefully taking into account the rights of the poor and the rights of nature.

Were our government for the *people*, we would have the best education in the world, universal health insurance, a decent way of financing elections, and a massive commitment to sources of clean energy.

If eternal life is on both sides of the grave, then to yearn for the future with no concern for the present is wrong. Heaven—and Hell—begin here and now, both for individuals and for nations, in what theologians call "realized eschatology." So the Spirit of God is always moving, prompting us ever more urgently to disarm the nations and empower the weak.

In his time on earth Jesus "stood tall," but not by making others cringe. He had power, but used it solely to empower others. He healed, but with no strings attached. He competed with none, loved all, even when we were least lovable, even to the point of dying for us on the cross. Walking with Jesus we can no longer be heartless, heedless in our haste to "join the general scramble and pant with the money-making street." Scales of heedlessness fall from our eyes. We see ourselves walking not alone with our Lord, but with all the peoples of the world whom we now view as fellow walkers, not as those who fall in behind. And all are marching to Zion, to the mountain of God, where—can anyone doubt it?—God will cause the nations to beat their swords into plowshares and return to the people the peace that only God could give and no nation had the right to take away.

Patriotism

O beautiful for pilgrim feet, whose
stern, impassioned stress
A thoroughfare for freedom beat
across the wilderness.
America, America, God mend thine
every flaw,
Confirm thy soul in self-control,
thy liberty in law.
                    —*Katharine Lee Bates*

Your heart was proud because of your beauty;
*   you corrupted your wisdom for*
the sake of your splendor.
        —*Ezekiel 28:17, describing proud Tyre*

*W*hen he emerged from Constitution Hall, Benjamin Franklin was recognized by a woman who asked of him, "What kind of government are you giving us?" "A republic, Madam, if you can keep it."

———— ⧉ ————

Hardly anyone in the world believes territorial discrimination to be as evil as racial or religious discrimination. But it is. Nationalism, at the expense of another nation, is just as wicked as racism at the expense of another race. In other words, good patriots are not nationalists. A nationalist is a bad patriot.

———— ⧉ ————

"Love of country is a wonderful thing, but why should love stop at the border?" (Pablo Casals).

—— ⤳ ——

All nations make decisions based on self-interest and then defend them in the name of morality.

—— ⤳ ——

Where is the "causa confessions," the point where one puts loyalty to God above obedience to the national will? For obedience to the law is no invariable obligation for those who must serve God rather than man. We said this to the Germans at Nuremberg; we must repeat it to ourselves now.

—— ⤳ ——

Christians forget that it was the Devil who tempted Jesus with unbounded wealth and power. And it is the Devil in every American that makes us feel good about being so powerful.

—— ⤳ ——

I think we can say that democracy is a form of government that demands more virtue of its citizens than any other form of government, but I do not think we can say that democracy guarantees that the virtue will be exercised. So let us term freedom of choice less a virtue than a necessity, a precondition to real freedom, which is the ability to make choices that are generous, loving, and wise. Our wills are not free when they will what is bigoted, narrow, ungenerous. Our wills are only free when they can will the will of a loving God. "Thy will be done on earth."

It is gratifying for Americans to recall that ours is the longest-lived revolution in the world, maybe even the most successful. But it would be a mistake to forget that our influence as a people was greatest when as a nation we were weakest. We rallied far more hopes and energies when we had no rockets and no muscle. The other day I read words of Alexander Hamilton more pertinent perhaps to our time than to his: "To be more safe the nations at length become willing to run the risk of being less free." Today our danger may lie in becoming more concerned with defense than with having things worth defending.

When there's doubt, there's more considered faith. Likewise, when citizens doubt, patriotism becomes more informed. For Christians to render everything to Caesar—their minds, their consciences—is to become evangelical nationalists. That's not a distortion of the gospel; that's desertion.

It's wonderful to love one's country, but faith is for God. National unity too is wonderful—but not in cruelty and folly.

"America, love it or leave it." I believe that. The trouble with that slogan, which found its way onto endless bumpers during the Vietnam War, was that it didn't mean what it said. It meant "America, *obey* it or leave it," as if national unity were more patriotic than national debate, especially when that unity seems to many to be based on folly. If the American people are worth the salt I think they're worth, they will never be politically united, for as Barbara Tuchman recently wrote, "A nation in consensus is a nation ready for the grave." Love of country, like love of parents, is never to be equated with blind obedience, as Jesus himself in both cases so poignantly demonstrated.

I only trust sad soldiers, as I only trust sad revolutionaries. Enthusiastic ones are always out to get someone.

Our mortal enemy is war, war itself. Let us not argue that we must go to war to defend selfish interests. They are not worth it. Nor let us argue that we must go to war to defend our democratic way of life. Such a way of life will not survive. And let us proclaim a new kind of patriotism, which takes as its object of ultimate loyalty not the nation-state, but the human race. (Didn't Margaret Mead say, "We have explored the entire planet and found only one human race"?)

"To sin by silence when they should protest, makes cowards of human beings" (Abraham Lincoln).

—— ⊱ ——

Sacrifice in and of itself confers no sanctity. Even—God forbid—if half a million of our boys were to die in Vietnam, that would not make the cause one whit more sacred. Yet we realize how hard that knowledge is to appropriate when one's loved one is numbered among the sacrificed.

—— ⊱ ——

How do you love America? Don't say, "My country, right or wrong." That's like saying, "My grandmother, drunk or sober"; it doesn't get you anywhere. Don't just salute the flag, and don't burn it either. Wash it. Make it clean.

How do you love America? With the vision and compassion of Christ, with a transcendent ethic that alone can fulfill "the patriot's dream that sees beyond the years, her alabaster cities gleam undimmed by human tears" (Katharine Lee Bates).

"Behold I make all things new," saith the Lord. Our revolutionary forebears seemed to understand that. They didn't bestir themselves to salvage the past. Their political debate pitted one kind of future against another kind of future. They knew people were supposed to die *to* an old order and not *with* the old order. How ironic that their descendants should today be crushed by ancient outmoded structures because we prefer to be victims than to be rebels! How ironic that the descendants of Thomas Jefferson should make like George III! How ironic that there's hardly a youth in the land as radical and as reasonable as was Ben Franklin in his eighties, and in his cups!

------ ⌘ ------

There are three kinds of patriots, two bad, one good. The bad ones are the uncritical lovers and the loveless critics. Good patriots carry on a lover's quarrel with their country, a reflection of God's lover's quarrel with all the world.

------ ⌘ ------

Let us dare to see that the survival unit in our time is no longer an individual nation or an individual anything. The survival unit in our time and henceforth is the whole human race and its environment.

------ ⌘ ------

The United States doesn't have to lead the world; it has first to join it. Then, with greater humility, it can play a wiser leadership role.

------ ⌘ ------

Individuals and nations are at their worst when, persuaded of their superior virtue, they crusade against the vices of others. They are at their best when they claim their God-given kinship with all humanity, offering prayers of thanks that there is more mercy in God than sin in us.

———— ⊱ ————

So where then in America does God dwell today?

I would say that God dwells with those in America who feel geographically at home and spiritually in exile. God dwells with them for going about doing good, repairing a broken world, for opposing America's entrenched fondness for subjugating nature in the name of progress and for keeping the faith despite the evidence, knowing that only in so doing has the evidence any chance of changing.

God dwells with those who seek God's face, those who may doubt the quality of the bread but don't kid themselves they are not hungry.

God dwells with every committed Jew, Moslem, Christian, Buddhist, Hindu who believes religious pluralism to be God's will, but who knows, as did Rabbi Heschel, that "the first and most important prerequisite of interfaith is faith." It is so easy in a time of paucity of faith for interfaith to become a substitute for faith, suppressing authenticity for the sake of compromise.

God dwells I'm sure with all who in wonder, reverence, and gratitude sing a new song in verse or prose, music and art, seeking to end the self-deception that tempts us all.

War and Peace

The war horse is a vain hope for victory,
and by its great might it cannot save.
—Psalm 33:17

Cure thy children's warring madness,
Bend our pride to thy control;
Shame our wanton selfish gladness
Rich in things and poor in soul.
—Harry Emerson Fosdick

War is a coward's escape from the problems of peace.
—Thomas Mann

*W*ar is always cause for remorse, never for exhilaration.

—— ⊰⊱ ——

Peace always seems a weary way off. As Jeremiah lamented, "We looked for peace, but no peace came." But to give up on peace is to give up on God.

—— ⊰⊱ ——

War is humanity's most chronic and incurable disease. Said Plato, "Only the dead have seen an end to war." Historian Will Durant estimated that in all of human history only twenty-nine years can be described as free of war. And of all centuries, the one just past set records for bloodletting.

—— ⊰⊱ ——

The war against Iraq is as disastrous as it is unnecessary; perhaps in terms of its wisdom, justice, purpose, and motives, the worst war in American history. Of course we feel for the Iraqis so long and cruelly oppressed, and we support our military men and women; but we don't support their military mission. They were not called to defend America but rather to attack Iraq. They were not called to die for, but rather to *kill* for, their country, and in an illegal and unjust war opposed by the UN Security Council and virtually the entire world. What more unpatriotic thing could we have asked of our sons and daughters serving in the military?

Whereas economic *power* helped eventually to win World War II, the war against terrorism will finally only be won by economic *justice*. There is nothing metaphysical about terrorism. It springs from specific historical causes—political oppression and economic deprivation. Until these injustices and our complicity in their furtherance are faced, our escalating counterviolence will predictably result in more and more terrorists attacking more and more American institutions at home and abroad.

Come to think of it, attacking worldwide poverty could be our best defense policy. It certainly would marginalize extremists and slow down the recruitment of new terrorists.

Peace does not come rolling in on the wheels of inevitability. We can't just wish for peace. We have to will it, fight for it, suffer for it, demand it from our governments as if peace were God's most cherished hope for humanity, as indeed it is.

"We must think as people of action and act as people of thought" (Henri Bergson).

If you're at the edge of an abyss the only progressive step is backward!

It is not really the world but the human race that is fragile, and getting ever more so as it is far from certain that we care enough for future generations to pay the price for their survival.

Let us recall that wars begin in the mind. We have first to *think* others to death. You can't kill a brother. You can't kill a sister, a friend, a fellow human being. But you can kill a Marxist, a capitalist, a terrorist. You can kill a Red Menace, or a "shark of Wall Street." And we further prepare the mind to kill by using such juiceless jargon as "collateral damage."

It is consoling, of course, to view ourselves as models of rectitude and even more so as misunderstood models of rectitude. But simple honesty compels us to see that we are as other nations are. The trouble with saying, "The only thing that the other side understands is force" is that you have to behave as if the only thing you understand is force.

Think how a rich and powerful nation proclaims itself the "defender of freedom" throughout the world. But is it freedom we are defending? Is it not perhaps first and foremost the privileges freedom has brought to us, and to us as Americans more than to anyone else? Freedom, as Camus used to teach us, "isn't made up principally of privileges. It is made up especially of duties." And if in America freedom's duties held sway over freedom's privileges, then why were we not crying bloody murder at Batista before Castro, at Trujillo, at the overthrow of Juan Bosch, and at Samoza before the advent of the Sandinistas?

People in every generation have striven for power, the only difference being that ours has achieved it. This is "the century of total war" because this is "the age of omnipotence." What has happened is curious. You know the expression "A man's reach should exceed his grasp." That means our moral imagination should stretch beyond what we are able to do. Now the situation is reversed: what we are able to do is beyond the reach of our moral imagination. Our capacity to destroy is virtually unlimited. But our capacity to imagine, to feel, to respond, is, as always, limited. Thus we are able to do physically what we cannot grasp morally. We are living beyond our moral means. That is the heart of our problem.

----- ⟨≋⟩ -----

It's certain that no one has yet lost an election bombing Baghdad, Tripoli, Khartoum, or Belgrade. That's because these strikes represent minimal risk to American lives. Since Vietnam, Americans have wanted no more body bags. And the Persian Gulf War strongly suggested that victory could be ours by expending technological rather than personal resources.

But with each bombing run, we earn more enemies than we subdue. More and more we are becoming the authors of the terrorism of which we are also the target. To some Americans as well as to many more foreigners, there is something repulsive about an attitude that says, "We are free to kill your civilians but we don't want you to kill our military."

----- ⟨≋⟩ -----

After experiencing the horrors of the Vietnam War, certain American veterans proclaimed they couldn't believe in God any more, as if it had been the will of God that they should have been over there in the first place. It is not the will of God that any human being die in a war, on a battlefield, and it is no exaggeration to picture Christ between the opposing lines, every bullet and missile passing through his body.

Why does God let these things happen? Because God can't prevent them, love being self-restricting when it comes to power. If these human disasters grieve us, we can imagine how they break God's heart. But human disasters are the responsibility of human beings, not God. We can blame God only for giving us the freedom that, misused, makes these disasters inevitable. Often, I confess, I do blame God. I rail at God, saying, "Look, God, if you give an expensive watch to a small child and the child smashes it, who's at fault?" But I have to recognize that if love is the name of the game, freedom is the absolute precondition. God's love is self-restricting when it comes to power. The Christmas story, more than any other in the Bible, shows us that we are going to be helped by God's powerlessness—or God's love—not by God's power. The Christmas story shows us that God had to come to earth as the child of Joseph and Mary because freedom for the beloved demands equality with the beloved.

The Cold War was devastating to warm hearts. The divine commandment to love your enemy was changed into an imperative to hate all Communists. Hatred became a patriotic virtue. We became more and more ignorant of things we were most assured.

Oh, how our Risen Lord must scorn the insolence and arrogance of our leaders: the surmises that pass as dogmas, the prejudices they call solutions, the speculations on nuclear war they suck out of their thumbs. The poor may suffer the degradation of poverty, but the leaders of the United States and of the Soviet Union are threatened by degradation through power.

What irony, that our Lord should rise in a world about to become one vast burial ground. Talk about living in sin! God grant that on this Easter day we recognize that it is a sin merely to build a nuclear weapon.

------- ⬧ -------

Life is consequential. We are punished not so much *for* as *by* our sins. We do not so much break the Ten Commandments as we are broken on them. Consequential for us as individuals, life is even more so for the nations of this nuclear world. Hadn't we better learn to be merciful when we live at each other's mercy? If we do not learn to be meek, will there be any earth for anyone to inherit?

------- ⬧ -------

Life swings on an ethical hinge. If you loosen that hinge, all history, and even nature, will feel the shock. For God is not mocked, and the kingdom of God comes through God's judgment, which promises the eventual downfall of every other kind of kingdom.

------- ⬧ -------

Many of God's lessons are based on St. Augustine's insight: "Never fight evil as if it were something that arose totally outside of yourself."

------- ⬧ -------

In the sight of our Risen Lord the mere possession of nuclear weapons must be an abomination comparable to the possession of slaves 150 years ago. And just as the object then was not to humanize but to abolish the institution of slavery, so today it is our Christian duty to abolish from the face of the earth every last nuclear weapon.

———— ⤳ ————

God alone has the authority to end life on the planet; all human beings have is the power. Since this power is so clearly not authorized by any tenet of the faith, Christians have to say that it is a sin not only to use, not only to threaten to use, but to *build* a nuclear weapon. In repentance lies our hope, the hope that we can recognize the crisis before it is validated by disaster.

———— ⤳ ————

Here in America we believe that our ability to make nuclear weapons is tantamount to a right to make them. We also believe, in this land of Adam Smith, that our ability to make money is also tantamount to a right to make endless amounts of it. But we have only the ability, not the right, to end life on this planet—only God has the authority to do that; and we have only the ability and not the right to gain more and more possessions for ourselves; that is if "the earth is the Lord's and the fullness thereof," and we believe in a Lord who proclaims, "Let justice roll down like mighty waters."

———— ⤳ ————

For men and women in a nuclear world, when the human race has outgrown war but hardly knows it yet, Jesus more than ever is the best way to liberation, freedom, and peace. The hostility that churned up Cain and that others throughout the centuries have sought to perpetuate, Jesus seeks to ground. That makes it our calling to ground, not to perpetuate, hostility. The violence stops here, with each one of us who claims Christ's holy name. The gossip, the false witness borne against a neighbor, the cold unconcern for warm human beings—all forms of violence, everything that violates human nature—stops with us.

———

It's not them and us; it's just us. And all of us are careening toward nuclear war. In World War II, six million Jews were herded into boxcars, stripped, shot or gassed, and incinerated in ovens all over Eastern Europe. But on the trains the great majority never guessed their destiny. We're on such a train to an even greater incineration and haven't the eyes to perceive it.

———

Just as the first step toward the abolition of slavery was the abolition of the slave trade, so now the first step toward the eventual abolition of national arsenals should be the abolition of the arms trade. Sellers must be held as culpable as buyers.

———

What we and other nuclear powers are practicing is really nuclear apartheid. A handful of nations have arrogated to themselves the right to build, deploy, and threaten to use nuclear weapons while policing the rest of the world against their production. The nuclear bomb tests carried out by India and Pakistan were as predictable as they were terrible because nuclear apartheid has no more chance of succeeding than did racial apartheid in South Africa.

Nuclear apartheid is utopian and arrogant. It is a recipe for proliferation, a policy of disaster. That is why Kofi Annan repeatedly says, "*Global* nuclear disarmament must remain at the top of the UN agenda." Shouldn't nuclear disarmament also be at the top of the churches' agenda?

———— ⟳ ————

The abolition of nuclear weapons is not a desirable option but a compelling imperative. And while it is a matter of conscience, it is no less a matter of profound self-interest. God is not mocked: what is grossly immoral can never in the long run be politically expedient.

———— ⟳ ————

We are beginning to resemble extinct dinosaurs who suffered from too much armor and too little brain.

———— ⟳ ————

How can we Americans claim to be a responsible power when we profess humane ideals and threaten unlimited slaughter? How could the then Soviet Union claim to be a responsible power when they and we together for forty-odd years, in the sacred name of deterrence, engaged in a nuclear arms race so open-ended that the world became as a prisoner in a cell condemned to death, awaiting the uncertain moment of execution?

——— ⟨⟩ ———

Just as a fat person cannot talk persuasively to a skinny one about the virtues of not overeating, so nuclear powers cannot convince nonnuclear ones to renounce access to nuclear weapons—not until the nuclear powers themselves start seriously to disarm. Either they disarm or they must face the fact that any nation in the world that wants nuclear weapons eventually will get them. Either the world becomes nuclear free or the whole planet becomes a nuclear porcupine.

——— ⟨⟩ ———

Universal prohibition is presently a cause at odds with conventional wisdom. But if nuclear war comes, all humanity will be downwind.

——— ⟨⟩ ———

Even if, by the grace of God, we succeed in ridding the earth of weapons of mass destruction, the ability to make them will forever and ever be part of the storehouse of human knowledge. Of all thoughts about the world's future, few are more sobering, for it

would be utterly naive to believe that a nation at war would grace-
fully choose to go down to defeat rather than reconstruct nuclear
weapons had it the ability to do so. In other words, having bitten the
nuclear apple there is no returning to innocence. It's hard not to con-
clude that humanity has outlived war—but doesn't know it.

———— ⋙ ————

Presently the United States spends on defense as much as the next
fifteen nations combined. Our troops are stationed in seventy-five
countries.

———— ⋙ ————

"And now abide faith. . . ." The abiding faith this country needs
for its spiritual restoration and future health is the faith of the
prophets, the prophets who loved Israel, but whose love for their
country was often measured by their deep disappointment with it.
Prophetic faith is full of anger, yet it is always anchored in the greatness and goodness of God, not in hatred of enemies. Prophetic faith
recognizes that economic tyranny can be as great as political tyranny.
Prophetic faith sees justice as central, not ancillary, to salvation. It
recognizes that God's unconditional concern for justice is not an
anthropomorphism (a projection upon God of our human attributes), but rather that our concern for justice is a theomorphism: to
the degree that we embody justice, God takes form within us.
   For American liberty to be restored and extended, American
Christians need to carry on with their country the same lovers' quarrel that the prophets of old carried on with Israel, and that God con-
sistently carries on with the whole world. We must say Yes to what
we can, and No to what we must. We must see that when a government betrays the ideals of a country, it is an act of loyalty to oppose

the government. We must take the road less traveled and be more concerned with our country saving its soul than with it losing face. "I tremble for my country when I recall that God is just" (Thomas Jefferson).

------ ⬥ ------

Rarely can majority rule be equated with the rule of conscience. Think of the long years during which the majority of American citizens supported slavery; think of the disenfranchisement of women, of child labor. Democracy is not based on the proven goodness of the people but on the proven evil of dictators. So the law never represents pure justice, but only about as much justice as any given people at any given time will sanction. In other words, the law *reflects* public opinion as much as it *instructs* public opinion. Therefore, if the law is to reflect more and reject less of humanity's highest notions about justice, someone has constantly to provoke change— the change new laws will serve to embody. Nonviolent civil disobedience, then, as practiced by Jesus, Socrates, Gandhi, and King, is not only an expression of conscience; it is a way to move society toward a greater measure of justice and mercy.

------ ⬥ ------

Certain questions need rigorously to be answered before undertaking any act of civil disobedience: how clear and great is the evil one hopes to oppose by civil disobedience? How hopeless is the remedy within the law? Is it possible to be disobedient without harm to innocent people? And what is the probable efficacy of the act—though this of course is a penultimate, never an ultimate consideration.

For further guidance, one is really driven to one's knees. To Peter, of course, all was illuminated inevitably and right, but for many of us, acts of civil disobedience will have to be undertaken with fear and trembling, perhaps out of a sense that not to disobey would be even worse.

------ ⟨≋⟩ ------

Pressure a man into civil disobedience and in the midst of the ensuing trouble he may have second thoughts and be embittered for life if the decision was not eminently his own. Pressure him away from civil disobedience, on the other hand, and he may feel for the rest of his life that he missed his one great moment of truth. (And after missing the first moment how much easier it is to miss so many others!)

------ ⟨≋⟩ ------

Jesus was more, not less, than a prophet; more, not less, political than others. Only his were the politics of eternity. And the politics of eternity insist not only on nonviolence—an affront to almost every revolutionary; they insist on "one world"—an affront to every nationalist. We shall begin to understand the politics of eternity when we recognize that territorial discrimination is as evil as racial discrimination.

------ ⟨≋⟩ ------

The trouble with violence is that it changes not too much, but too little. Nonviolence is more radical because it is more truthful. Violence always ends up calling on lies to defend it, just as lies call on violence to defend them. By contrast, truth is naked, vulnerable as Christ, its only weapon Christ's own, God's love. So the very love of God that found oppression, poverty, and corruption intolerable, this same love, rather than inflict suffering—even on those imposing it on the poor—took suffering upon itself. What can only be said cynically of another—"It is better that one man should die than that an entire nation perish" (ah, the demands of national security!)—can be said in utter truthfulness about oneself: "It is better that I should die rather than a single other person perish." That's finally how truth disarms, and there is no better way.

Nature

The earth is the LORD'S
and all that is in it.
　　　　　—Psalm 24:1

I love thy rocks and rills,
Thy woods and templed hills
My heart with rapture thrills
Like that above.
　　　　　—Samuel Francis Smith

The larger the island of knowledge
The greater the shoreline of wonder.
　　　　　—Huston Smith

President Bush Jr. rightly spoke of an "axis of evil," but it is not Iran, Iraq, and North Korea. Here is a more likely trio calling for Herculean efforts to defeat: environmental degradation, pandemic poverty, and a world awash with weapons.

We have divorced nature from nature's God. We view nature essentially as a toolbox. Nature may have beauty but no purpose. I am convinced that unless in our own minds we re-wed nature to nature's God, we are not going to save our environment. Caution lest we exhaust our natural resources and kill ourselves in the process—that kind of caution is not enough. What we need beyond caution is reverence. What we need beyond practical fears are moral qualms. Unless nature is "re-sanctified" we will never see nature as worthy of ethical considerations similar to those that presently govern human relations. And I'm not at all optimistic. For not only are Christians poor stewards of God's creation; seriously challenging the Christian notion of "stewardship" are those who want us to think of ourselves as planet managers. And management today includes biotechnology, genetic engineering, a way to create new life. In conceptual and moral terms, genetic engineering may well be the most important scientific advance since the smashing of the atom. It suggests that if nature can't put up with our numbers and habits, well, we'll just have to change nature.

It is a great mistake to talk, as many political leaders do, of balancing the needs of the economy with those of the environment. An economy, national or world, is a subsystem of the ecosystem. Therefore we cannot speak of growth as an unquestioned good.

If indeed we are stewards of God's creation, Christians have a big role to play. And the results could be dramatic, for the environmental point of view turns us away from the possessive individualism that has long been our secular credo and toward the interdependency that alone can save us. It was one thing for people to consume nature's surpluses. Today we are destroying the productive base of both present and future surpluses. Only together, all together, can we save the base.

There are limits to growth. This has to effect our understanding of the biblical term "dominion." It is even possible that we have misconceived "dominion." For God doesn't exploit. God doesn't manipulate. It may well be that instead of exploiting we are going to have to conserve nature. Maintenance will have to replace the notion of progress. Nurturing will have to replace the notion of engineering. A new doctrine of stewardship will have to become more important than doctrines of ownership—that is, if we are to stop devouring our planet, spewing out wastes in all directions. And the new doctrine of stewardship will have to go hand in hand with the old doctrine of social justice, for in an age of scarcity the question of equity can no longer be deferred. Needed is a soulful kinship with the land and with each other.

It may be that as civilization advances, the sense of wonder declines. But it is ironic that just as technology frees us to be full human beings, not mere survivors of the earth's rigors, at this very moment we may be about to lose the whole planet because we have lost our sense of wonder. For finally only reverence can restrain violence, violence against nature, violence against one another.

What is the use of a house if you haven't a tolerable planet to put it on? Our nation is going to have quite a lot to say about how tolerable this planet is going to be. And if it's as hard for a rich individual to get into the kingdom of God as it is for a camel to pass through the eye of a needle, you can imagine what it must be like for a rich nation!

If you believe, as many believers do, in a politically engaged spirituality, and you're trying to save the environment; if you are persuaded that economic crimes can cause damage as extensive as the crimes of violence so endemic in the world today; and if you're an American trying to temper patriotic fervor with a healthy dose of national humility, you're bound at times to feel like quitting. But if Jesus never allowed his soul to be cornered into despair, and if it was to those furthest from the seats of power that he said, "You are the salt of the earth. . . .you are the light of the world"—who then are we to quit "fighting the good fight of faith"?

Life in General

Return, O my soul, to your rest,
    for the LORD *has dealt bountifully with you.*
For you have delivered my soul from death,
    my eyes from tears,
    my feet from stumbling.
                                    —Psalm 116:7–8

I need thy presence every passing hour;
What but thy grace can spoil the tempter's power?
Who, like thyself, my guide and stay can be?
Through cloud and sunshine, Lord, abide with me.
                                    —Henry Francis Lyte

he pursuit of truth" rightly implies that a gap exists between ourselves and truth. But what's hidden and evasive? Is it we or truth? Maybe it is we who evade truth's quest for us.

---- ≋ ----

Relationships—not facts and reason—are the key to reality. By entering those relationships, knowledge of reality is unlocked (Parker Palmer).

---- ≋ ----

Let's not forget how great artists define meaning. Procrastination has not been the same since Hamlet, or jealousy since Othello, or opportunistic ambition since Macbeth. Or consider this: Thoreau read Wordsworth; John Muir read Thoreau; Teddy Roosevelt read John Muir; and the results were national parks. It took a century, but hopefully we'll have them for centuries more!

---- ≋ ----

It's a heavy responsibility to be a parent. But we kid ourselves when we celebrate our freedoms without realizing that it is our obligations that give our lives their meaning. Children are the anchors that hold us to life. Chubby children clinging to our necks keep us low and wise!

Simply having children, however, does not make mothers. Nor, as I suggested, do you have to have children in order to mother. "Whoever does the will of God is my brother and sister and mother." All of us are called to love each other into all God made and meant us to be.

----- ⊗ -----

Some people think that to do something truly evil you have to be some kind of Bengal tiger. In fact, it is enough to be a tame tabby, a nicely packaged citizen, safe, polite, obedient, and sterile. It's enough to be a nice guy, as opposed to a good man.

----- ⊗ -----

No one need be afraid of fear, only afraid that fear will stop him or her from doing what's right. Courage means being well aware of the worst that can happen, being scared almost to death, and then doing the right thing anyhow.

----- ⊗ -----

Have you ever noticed how Jesus healed with no strings attached? He didn't say to blind Bartimaeus, now healed, "Now don't you go ogling beautiful women." To the owner of the withered hand he restored, Jesus didn't warn, "No stealing now."

―― ⨠ ――

You can steel yourself against death and in general against the hardships of life, but in so doing you wall out the very support you really need. "The one thing a clenched fist can't do is accept a helping hand" (Frederick Buechner).

―― ⨠ ――

Clearly the trick in life is to die young as late as possible.

―― ⨠ ――

It does seem to be the case, in the long if not in the short run, that life gives back what we pour into it. Those who consider the world unfriendly are apt themselves to be pretty unfriendly.

―― ⨠ ――

One shouldn't be too upset about the way the ball bounces if one has dropped it oneself.

------- ⟨≋⟩ -------

I believe the power of God is lodged in the very marrow of our substance and is pressing, constantly pressing, for release in order to permeate every fiber of our being. And the demand is not for self-denial, as is so often preached, but rather for self-discovery and self-realization, which includes the commitment to God that is the final fulfillment of human life. This I think is what St. Paul means when he says, "God searches our inmost being" and "The kingdom of God consists not in words but in power." To think we can escape wrestling with this power is to dream.

------- ⟨≋⟩ -------

There is in other words a difference between having a friend and being a friend, between having success and being successful, between getting an education and becoming learned. If we use knowledge, music, art, sports, and eminently others—if we use them just to enrich ourselves, then paradoxically we impoverish ourselves, at least at our very core. For all things then become as clothes: they cover but they do not touch or develop our inner being, and we become as those who believe they can only become visible when something visible covers the surface.

But if we give ourselves to art, music, sports, knowledge, and eminently to others, then we experience that biblical truth that "he who loses his life shall find it," shall find life being fulfilled, and find that joy is self-fulfillment, self-fulfillment is joy.

For joy is to escape from the prison of selfhood and to enter by love into union with the life that dwells and sings within the essence of every other thing and in the core of our own souls. Joy is to feel the doors of the self fly open into a wealth that is endless because none of it is ours and yet it all belongs to us.

———— ⌘ ————

We put our best foot forward, but it's the other one that needs the attention.

———— ⌘ ————

The only form of suffering that can't possibly put us in closer touch with nature and all living creatures is the suffering of a bruised ego. Always self-centered, pride is never more so than when it is hurt. But other forms of suffering can produce selfless courage. They can widen our circle of compassion, putting us in closer touch with those who suffer as we do and far more, the world around— provided our own lives are rooted and grounded in the secure knowledge of God's love for us. Only by knowing "the love of Christ which surpasses knowledge" can we in cloud and sunshine pass on the riches of that love.

———— ⌘ ————

Envy provides one of the best commentaries on human nature, for it is the only one of the so-called seven deadly sins that has no gratification at all. Lust and gluttony can claim some immediate gratification. But not envy. Yet that sin, which can offer only endless self-torment, can hold us faster than any other.

There is in this world an element of tragedy in choice. We are asked to choose not only between good and evil but between goods, and to follow a great good means the sacrifice of lesser ones. But sacrifice can be beautiful if we understand both the greater good and the beauty of the thing being sacrificed. What is so terrible is to scorn pleasure in the way pleasure is so often scorned by sourpuss, austere ascetics. But it is a very different thing gently to lay aside a pleasure recognizing that a lot of things have gently to be laid aside in this world if we are to seek the pearl of great price.

The devil is always suggesting that we compromise our high calling by substituting the good in place of the best.

None of the twelve disciples had any of the so-called "advantages"—education, wealth, social status. They were as ordinary as they come, which makes the point that Christ is not looking for extraordinary people but for *ordinary* men and women who do ordinary things extraordinarily well.

———— ⪧ ————

The worst thing we can do with a dilemma is to resolve it prematurely because we haven't the courage to live with uncertainty.

———— ⪧ ————

Maybe we're stalled in our journey because we engage in unproductive nostalgia. We yearn for the good old days, which seem to us better only because we ourselves were better.

———— ⪧ ————

There are people who say Jesus was never tempted, never really, because he never ceded to temptation. But who knows better the strength of the enemy, he who surrenders or he who struggles to the end?

———— ⪧ ————

To take on the imperfections of the world means of course that your heart will be saddened, your self-confidence impaired, your trust disappointed. You will know despair. But isn't maturity the ability to surmount despair? Isn't that what growing up is all about— learning to outlast despair?

The longest, most arduous trip in the world is often the journey from the head to the heart. Until that round trip is completed, we remain at war with ourselves. And, of course, those at war with themselves are apt to make casualties of others, including friends and loved ones.

Our business in life is less making something of ourselves than finding something worth doing and losing ourselves in it.

Life being what it is, if we don't make a difference by trying, we'll make a difference by not trying.

You can no more rid the world of sinners than you can stock it with saints. As Sam Keen warned; "Every utopian scheme hides a Grand Inquisitor."

If it's immature to be childish, to remain childlike may be a function of maturity, for as Jesus said, "Whoever does not receive the kingdom of God as a little child will not enter therein." Discussing this passage, biblical commentators like to dwell on the natural humility, the basic obedient and trusting quality of children; and I have no quarrel with such emphasis. All of us could profit from being a little more humble, trusting, and obedient, although Christians have to recognize that obedience to God has more to do with being love abiding than law abiding. But why, I wonder, don't these same commentators talk about the natural idealism of children? It's children who want to save the seals, the whales, and all the rest of us to boot. It's kids who sell cookies for causes, bake bread for brotherhood, save pennies to fight pollution. It's kids who have walkathons against war. And of course we encourage them. We believe in their being generous. But it's also true that we encourage them to outgrow it, as though generosity were a pair of short pants. Do you think Jesus would bless that view of growing up?

Why should we want all things to enjoy life when we have been given life to enjoy all things?

God is the source of life; it is self-destructive to put our trust else-where. If giving causes more pain than pleasure, it is not our money but our faith that is insufficient.

—— ❧ ——

A wise person accepts the challenge of the darkness and develops a catlike ability to see at night. Such a person perceives that good and evil have an incestuous relationship; that nothing is easier than to denounce the evildoer, and nothing is more difficult than to under-stand him. It is of course emotionally satisfying to denounce ene-mies. God knows it is emotionally satisfying to be righteous with that righteousness that nourishes itself in the blood of sinners. But God also knows that what is emotionally satisfying can also be spir-itually devastating. And it is spiritually devastating to claim more light than is shed by God upon the human situation and to project a brief, narrow vision of life as eternal truth. Life doesn't sit around to have its portrait painted, and besides, who could ever catch its shimmering depths?

—— ❧ ——

I am a little clearer now on the issue of hypocrisy. Of course we all pass ourselves off as something we are not, but not *anything* we are not. Generally we try to pass ourselves off as something that is special in our hearts and minds, something we yearn for, something beyond us. That's rather touching.

—— ❧ ——

It's comforting to be bitter about evil—not creative, but comforting. It's also easy to blame everything on a tragedy. But in my experience most people give up on life not because of a tragedy, but because they no longer see joys worth celebrating; they do not see that human life, under any circumstances, never ceases to have meaning. Tragedy offers the opportunity to find new meaning and most of all to reevaluate what's important.

— ⟨⟩ —

There is an enormous discrepancy between what we are brought up to believe and what American society rewards as belief. Talk about the cussedness of the race! It's money that measures the success or failure of most of the games we play most of our lives. It's money that gives us our identity, compared to which our identity in God is but a footnote. We expect more from financial success than from our relationship with God.

— ⟨⟩ —

"If anyone strikes you on the right cheek, turn the other also." This doesn't mean, however, that we're supposed to be doormats for others to walk on with hobnailed boots. It's my experience that people seldom want to walk over you until you lie down, so it's better to stay standing. Turning the other cheek means "Be a lightning rod; ground the hostility." When you are insulted, call the other's attention to the hurt but do not retaliate in kind. Try—and believe me it is hard—try not even to resent it, for our job is to get *to* each other, not *at* each other. You know as well as I do that when enmities dim, lives glow all the stronger.

— ⟨⟩ —

The biblical view would seem to be this: the intellect is one of God's most beautiful gifts. It can hardly be overtrained. Good intentions are never enough. An excited but uninformed citizen is a menace. But the mind is finally only an instrument, and it makes a whale of a difference if it is at the service of a fearful or a loving person.

If indeed we love the Lord with all our hearts, minds, and strength, we are going to have to stretch our hearts, open our minds, and strengthen our souls, whether our years are three score and ten or not yet twenty. God cannot lodge in a narrow mind. God cannot lodge in a small heart. To accommodate God, they must be palatial.

Often in life, when we find ourselves in binds, we choose the path of least resistance, or maybe we refuse to choose. When we need to be most decisive, we go passive. I think that you have to be good by choice and that much evil is simply a refusal to choose. In fact, most evil in this world probably stems from indecision. This is an important point to make in a country that makes much of freedom of choice. For what is freedom of choice if you've lost the ability to choose?

To refuse to take refuge in conformity is an admirable form of defiance. But freedom, which likewise rejects conformity, also accepts with grace the inevitable limitations of life. And Albert Camus was surely right to insist that the one true freedom is to come to terms with death.

Nothing separates us more from God and our fellow human beings than our grievances. If you want to avoid God, concentrate on money, status, health, but most of all on your grievances.

Had Jesus heeded both his parents and the religious authorities of his day, instead of saving the world he would have become the best carpenter in Nazareth. Were our children to heed us and the religious authorities of our day, they'd all become nicely packaged citizens—safe, polite, and obedient.

All of us know, or should have experienced many times in our lives, the conflict between a narrow, safe loyalty and loyalty to God—the conflict between loyalty to our family and loyalty to the world, our larger family. For Jesus the conflict was apparently so intense that it could finally be resolved only at the very end of his life, and only on a cross: "Woman, behold your son. Son, behold your mother."

That in this moment of pain Jesus could be so filial is indeed deeply moving. Apparently Joseph is dead; Mary is widowed, and Jesus is providing for her physical and economic well-being. But beyond that, he is providing for her spiritual well-being in a very interesting way. Now Mary too leaves her family and goes to John; and by urging her to join his disciple, Jesus includes her in his mission, thereby resolving the conflict between loyalty to her and loyalty to God.

Things to be well aware of:

"The narcissism of minor differences" (Freud).

A dog can't go anywhere if he's always stopping to scratch his fleas.

Not all roads lead to the peak of the same mountain; some lead over the precipice.

God's forgiveness is more than a blessing; it's a challenge.

Things not worth doing are not worth doing well.

→ "The highest reward for human toil is not what we get for it, but what we become by it" (John Ruskin).

To let a point pass that calls for a challenge is to be politely dishonest.

The simplest act of human kindness for a fellow human being is more important than any refinement of the mind.

Fear is the enemy of learning; it gives ignorance its power.

God loves us as we are, but much too much to leave us there.

"Our doubts are traitors
    And make us lose the good we oft might win,
    By fearing to attempt" (Shakespeare).

There never was a night or a problem that could defeat sunrise or hope.

The Church

God of grace and God of glory
On thy people pour thy power;
Crown thine ancient church's story,
Bring her bud to glorious flower.
Grant us wisdom, grant us courage,
For the facing of this hour
For the facing of this hour.
　　　　　—Harry Emerson Fosdick

　　Caring is the greatest thing,
　　Caring matters most.
　　　　　—Baron von Hügel

*I*t is often said that the Church is a crutch. Of course it's a crutch. What makes you think you don't limp?

----- ❧ -----

What's the point of being Christian if you don't also know that what God withholds in the way of protection, he more than supplies in the form of support. For the world breaks God's heart, too. No pain our spirits endure, no weakness that impairs our bodies, no grief that bows us low fails to find its counterpart in God who, as we see, in Christ suffers with and for us. "He that keepeth Israel shall neither slumber or sleep." Sometimes I think it's God's pain, not God's peace, that passes all understanding. So come home to church, not for protection against all the travails of this earth, but rather for all the support that heaven alone can provide. Finally, come to leave. For we come to God's house, to this open house, to find love and to defeat hate, in order that the world itself can become an open house.

----- ❧ -----

I know it is hard for a middle-class preacher and his middle-class congregation to identify themselves readily with the multitudes. But what we must realize is that a multitude can be middle class as well as proletarian, capitalistic as well as communistic. The multitudes grouped around the cross represent any group in which the herd element dominates, any group whose members can no longer judge individually nor act freely. And respectability and good manners and efficiency can be hallmarks of the herd mentality just as easily as bad manners and inefficiency.

Of course the Church is conservative for it has so much to conserve. But let it conserve a vision of the world's destiny and not the structures of the world's past. Let the Church in remembering Christ remember that it is conserving the most uprooting, the most revolutionary force in all human history. For it was Christ who crossed every boundary, broke down every barrier. He crossed the boundaries of class by eating with the outcasts. He crossed the boundary of nations by pointing to a Samaritan as the agent of God's will. He transgressed religious boundaries by claiming the Sabbath was made for man and not man for the Sabbath. Everywhere he manifested his freedom and called others to theirs, calling them forth from family, national, and religious loyalties to loyalty to the world at large. If ever there was a man who trusted his origins and had the courage to emerge from them, it was Christ.

This tarnished but still glittering wonder of God's creation is worth fighting for. Kindness that seeks at all costs to avoid trouble is not Christian. Yes, we know it in our own lives—God must afflict the comfortable before he can comfort the afflicted. Why then, we may ask in God's name, is the Church in this country placating, entertaining, reverently rearranging minutiae when knowledge for salvation for a confused, inert, and frightened people has been put into her mouth to proclaim?

And all hands are needed to save this sinking ship. Let Christians not quibble about commitments to Christ. Let all those who want to keep civilization civilized—put quality into culture, humanity into business, life into the millions who are now drifting—let them all be drawn to the cause and then if they will, let them find Christ as the leader who can achieve it.

It behooves us North American Christians to realize now what the German churches learned too late some forty years ago: it is not enough to resist with confession; we must confess with resistance.

The Church, of all the institutions in society, interprets the memory and proclaims the message of the coming kingdom. The Church may distort Jesus into a white middle-class pillar of American respectability; it may pervert his image into that of a religious Babbitt pushing the cult of successfulness; it may distort and pervert his image, but the Church cannot forget Jesus. And in spite of its best efforts to domesticate that Jesus, the Church knows and frequently fears that his message will be rediscovered. The Church cannot help but keep the name in circulation, and where the name is remembered there is hope.

The Eucharist quenches my thirst for hope.

————— ≋ —————

At Riverside Church during infant baptism, I take the baby in my arms and say, "Little child, for you Jesus Christ came, he struggled, he suffered; for you he endured the darkness of Gethsemane, the anguish of Calvary; for you he triumphed over death, and you, little child, know nothing of all this. But thus is confirmed the word of the Apostle: 'We love God because God first loved us.'"

Then, in baptizing the child, I state the name and say, "I baptize thee in the name of the Father, of the Son and of the Holy Spirit, one God, mother of us all."

————— ≋ —————

A church is a place where we try to think, speak, and act in God's way, not in the way of a fear-filled world. A church is a home for love, a home for brothers and sisters to dwell in unity, to rest and be healed, to let go their defenses and be free—free from worries, free from tensions, free to laugh, free to cry.

————— ≋ —————

Most church boats don't like to be rocked; they prefer to lie at anchor rather than go places in stormy seas. But that's because we Christians view the Church as the object of our love instead of the subject and instrument of God's. Faith cannot be passive; it has to go forth—to assault the conscience, excite the imagination. Faith fans the flames of creativity altogether as much as it banks the fires of sin.

Too many Christians seek an all-powerful God so that we might be weak when God Himself in Christ became weak that we might become strong. Still others—fundamentalists, for example—longing to be spared the insecurity of uncertainty, engage in what psychiatrists call "premature closure." They misuse faith as a substitute for thought, when faith, in fact, is what makes good thinking possible. Still other church members suffer defeat at the hands of the world. But instead of turning their defeat into the occasion for the victory God always had in mind for them, they try to compensate for their defeat by seizing turf in the church and holding onto it for dear life.

Local churches, ministers, and laity alike need to be prodded, for we domesticate God's word too soon. Lacking the vigor to deal with big problems, we allow ourselves to become mesmerized by little ones.

No church that understands itself as a stranger in an alien country can be for the status quo. Too many churches preach Christ separated from the kingdom that Christ himself preached. Too many

Christians will today pray, "Thy kingdom come," and tomorrow bar its way. Those who attack the status quo are not mixing religion with politics as much as those who support it. Two years ago, in this church, Dom Helder Camara, bishop of Recife, Brazil, a friend of the poor and therefore at serious odds with his government, was asked by a reporter if he wasn't mixing religion with politics. Answered the bishop; "When the Roman Catholic Church is in bed with government, no one says, 'the Church is mixing religion with politics.'"

And of course churches should quarrel far more with the governments of their own countries. The prophets of Israel dwelt as little on the sins of Assyria, which were manifold, as did Jesus on the evils of Rome. Likewise in this church we shouldn't dwell on the sins of the Soviet Union, which also are manifold. None of the terrible things done by the Soviet government are done in the name of a single American, whereas the American government can do nothing except in the name of every American.

What finally counts is not what biblical texts or church doctrines tell us we *may* believe, but what humanity, reason, justice, and Christ's love tell us we *ought* to believe.

It seems to me that in joining a church you leave home and home town to join a larger world. The whole world is your new neighborhood and all who dwell therein—black, white, yellow, red, stuffed and starving, smart and stupid, mighty and lowly, criminal and self-respecting, American or Russian—all become your sisters and brothers in the new family formed in Jesus. By joining a church you declare your individuality in the most radical way in order to affirm community on the widest possible scale.

———— ❦ ————

Churches have a special obligation to point out that "God 'n country" is not one word, and to summon America to a higher vision of its meaning and destiny.

———— ❦ ————

I look to the religious community in America to persuade Americans that we have sold our birthright of freedom and justice for a mess of national security. National security—which says, "I can only preserve the security of my country by threatening the security of yours"—must give way to something a little more in tune with the religious vision: common security, which insists no one is safe unless all are safe.

———— ❦ ————

There are those who prefer certainty to truth, those in church who put the purity of dogma ahead of the integrity of love. And what distortion of the gospel it is to have limited sympathies and unlimited certainties, when the very reverse—to have limited certainties and unlimited sympathies—is not only more tolerant but far more Christian.

———— ⟨⟩ ————

In Christ's sight, there are no insiders and outsiders, for we are finally of one nature and one flesh and one grief and one hope. And in Christ's sight, if we fail in love we fail in all things else, which probably means that faults of passion are less deplorable than the cooler faults we tend to minimize.

———— ⟨⟩ ————

The stumbling block for most sensitive nonbelievers is not Christ but Christians, not God but suffering and the fact that the church in its hour of prosperity has worked so little for its alleviation.

———— ⟨⟩ ————

The only security in life lies in embracing its insecurity. And faith in Jesus Christ, far from diminishing the risks, inspires the courage to take them on—all of them, including the risk of intellectual uncertainty.

———— ⟨⟩ ————

It is important that our churches be courageous and creative, not sanctuaries for frightened Americans, which is to say recruiting grounds for authoritarian figures and movements that bear the earmarks of an emerging fascism.

Many of us Christians who feel so at home in our churches may, in fact, be miles away from God. As Karl Barth observed, "Many people go to church to make their last stand against God."

It is a mistake to look to the Bible to close a discussion; the Bible seeks to open one. God leads with a light rein, giving us our head. Jesus spoke in parables because these stories have a way of shifting responsibility from the narrator to the hearer. Christians have to listen to the world as well as to the Word—to science, to history, to what reason and our own experience tell us. We do not honor the higher truth we find in Christ by ignoring truths found elsewhere.

What must a prophetic minority do? Essentially, as did Jeremiah and all the prophets, speak truth to power. For governments are like individuals: they oversimplify the things that make them angry, and their ideological commitments distort their perceptions and deaden their moral sensibilities.

------ ⟨≋⟩ ------

We are called on not to mirror but to challenge culture, not to sustain but to upend the status quo, and if that to some sounds overly bold, isn't it true that God is always beckoning us toward horizons we aren't sure we want to reach?

------ ⟨≋⟩ ------

Many of us have a strong allergic reaction to change of any kind. The result is an intolerance for nonconforming ideas that runs like a dark streak through human history. In religious history this intolerance becomes particularly vicious when believers divide the world into the godly and the ungodly; for then, hating the ungodly is not a moral lapse but rather an obligation, part of the job description of being a true believer.

------ ⟨≋⟩ ------

The Bible knows nothing of a moral majority. It assumes that the individual conscience, as opposed to the mass mind, best reflects the universal conscience of humankind. And the Bible insists that a prophetic minority always has more to say to a nation than any majority, Silent, Moral, or any other. As a matter of fact, majorities in the Bible generally end up stoning the prophets, which suggests that democracies are based less on the proven goodness of the people than on the proven evil of dictators.

----- ❧ -----

If we are not as yet joined one to another in love, we most surely are in sin, and sin is a wonderful bond because it precludes the possibility of separation through judgment.

----- ❧ -----

I have never been persuaded by arguments against the ordination of women. The Vatican insists there were no women among the original twelve disciples. Well, there were also no Gentiles. And as a Roman Catholic once asked, "If Mary could carry our Lord and Savior in her body, why can't a woman carry his message on her lips?"

----- ❧ -----

If we're talking abut changing a society that yields most painfully to change, we are really talking about being good stewards not only in our vocations, but in the public realm. The important decisions in our time—whether there will be peace or war, freedom or totalitarianism, racial equality or discrimination, homophilia or homophobia, food or famine—all these are political decisions. To Christians, political decisions are not at the center of their faith; they are at the periphery of their faith. But without a periphery there can be no center. A center without a periphery is a contradiction in terms. Together, faith in Jesus Christ and political application of that faith form one unbroken circle.

When to stress their distinction and when to stress their unity depends almost entirely on the situation. Not every political issue of the day demands a decision from the churches, and I feel strongly that churches should not pursue political goals that are self-serving or parochial. I hate to see Christians try to legislate their convictions on divorce or abortion into state or federal law. I hate to see Christians fight to establish Sunday blue laws, or try to keep crèches on public greens, or prayer in and evolution out of public schools.

But I love to see Christians enter the fray on behalf of the poor and disadvantaged, to fight for housing for low-income families, for decent health care for the aging, for fair treatment for minorities, for peace for everyone—provided they always remember that there are many causes and more than one solution to problems of injustice and war. Most of all, in these times that are neither safe nor sane, I love to see Christians risk maximum fidelity to Jesus Christ when they can expect minimal support from the prevailing culture. I have in mind what the prophet Nathan did to King David—he spoke truth to power.

A central message of Christian life is this: ask Jesus for but a thimbleful of help and you get an oceanful in return.

Paradoxically it is in church that we learn how to live alone—to be free, strong, and mature—just as it is when we are alone that we realize how properly to live with others. There is an interesting relationship between being alone and being in community: "Let him who cannot be alone beware of community. . . . Let him who is not in community beware of being alone" (Bonhoeffer).

Church is where all hearts are one so that nothing else has to be one. Church is where there's such a climate of acceptance that each of us can be his or her unique self. Church is where we learn to be free, strong, and mature by sharing with one another our continued bondage, weakness, and immaturity. Church is where we so love one another that it becomes bearable to live as solitaries.

The central problem of the Christian church in America today is that most of us fear the cure more than the illness. Most of us prefer the plausible lie that we can't be cured to the fantastic truth that we can be. And there's a reason: if it's hell to be guilty, it's certainly scarier to be responsible—*response-able*, able to respond to God's visionary and creative love. No longer paralyzed, our arms would be free to embrace the outcast and the enemy, the most confirmed addict, the reddest of Soviet communists. No longer paralyzed, our feet would be free to walk out of any job that is harmful to others and meaningless to us, free even to walk that lonesome valley without fear of evil. Everything is possible to those whose eyes, no longer fixed on some status symbol or other, are held instead by the gaze of him who can dispense freedom and life in measures unheard of.

But as the hand of love freely extended always returns covered with scars (if not nailed to a cross), it is not dumb to refuse the cure; it is not dumb to remain paralyzed, stuck on the pallet; but it is *boring*. And alas, whether they occupy pulpits or sit in the pews, most American Christians are still on the pallet. Like the paralytic, they know they are sinners, at least in a vague sort of way. But lacking his will to be cured, lacking the courage to be well, they do not seek the forgiveness that offers a new way of life; instead, they seek punishment—which, by assuaging the guilt, makes the old way of life bearable anew. And they find this punishment not only in boring sermons and services, but also in a religion of legalism and moralism that turns people who could be free and loving into mean little Puritans, into blue-nosed busybodies.

Courage is a crucial virtue, for once again the currents of history are churning into rapids, threatening to carry before them everything we have loved, trusted, looked to for pleasure and support. We are being called upon to live with enormous insecurity. The churches could become centers of creative and courageous thinking. They could also become sanctuaries for frightened Americans, recruiting grounds for authoritarian figures and movements, some of which already bear the earmarks of an emerging fascism.

Will we be scared to death or scared to life? It all depends on where we find our ultimate security. In Leipzig, Martin Luther was asked, "Where will you be, Brother Martin, when church, state, princes, and people turn against you?" Answered Brother Martin, "Why then as now, in the hands of Almighty God."

I think disguise is the essence of evil. Doing an evil thing doesn't make a person evil. But calling the evil good, believing the disguise—that's when real trouble begins. And if disguise is the essence of evil, there is surely no better disguise than the cloak of religious piety. Never do people do evil so cheerfully as when they do it from religious conviction. The true miracle is that there is not more downright wickedness in all the religious institutions of the world.

------ ⊰≋⊱ ------

There is no eternal life for those who starve the poor. You can't be proud and Christian both. How God must despise the sounds of those who pray this day, "Thy kingdom come" and tomorrow bar its way. How God must despise the spectacle of Christians who climb upon the cross to be seen from afar, thereby trampling on the one who has hung there so long.

------ ⊰≋⊱ ------

It's wrong for preachers on every issue to stand as if at Armaggedon battling for the Lord. I know that tolerance is a tricky business. Some people actually think that tolerance means being so broadminded that your brains fall out. But I'm worried about growing intolerance in the church. I'm worried that the virtue of moral indignation is becoming the vice of moralism. Moralism is historically one of America's great defects. Moralism is intolerant of ambiguity, perceiving reality in extreme terms of good and evil and regarding more sophisticated judgments as soft and unworthy. The temptation to become moralistic is strong, for it is emotionally satisfying to have enemies rather than problems. It is emotionally satisfying to seek out culprits rather than flaws in the system. God knows it's emotionally satisfying to be righteous with that righteousness that nourishes itself in the blood of sinners. But God also knows that what is emotionally satisfying can also be spiritually devastating.

----- ⬦ -----

I remember several years ago a freshman asking if he could give me some advice. "Go ahead," I said. "Well, Sir, when you say something that is both true and painful, say it softly." Say it in other words to heal and not to hurt. Say it in love.

----- ⬦ -----

Preachers should be explorers as well as pulpit pounders. The energy that abounds in so many preachers, that glandular energy which so frequently is mistaken for the Holy Spirit—such energy is no substitute for wisdom; and wisdom abounds in Pascal's observation that a person "does not show his greatness by being at one extremity, but rather by touching both at once."

----- ⬦ -----

In contrast to many a preacher today, Jesus knew that "Love your enemies" didn't mean "Don't make any."

----- ⬦ -----

In almost every church there are gentle cowards who think their gentleness offsets their cowardice. It doesn't. Compassion frequently demands confrontation, as all those twentieth-century movements illustrate. The primary reason I suspect their views failed to prevail is because churches vastly prefer charity, which in no way affects the status quo, to justice, which immediately leads to political confrontation. Fellow pastors, be as pastoral as possible but never surrender ethical initiative!

I hope preachers would dare to take on the ambiguities of our time. Change today is coming on apace. The currents of history are churning into rapids, sweeping before them all the familiar buoys that long have marked the channels of our lives. And when we look at the Ship of State, ours or almost anybody else's, all we seem to see—and hear—is canvas tearing and cables parting. No wonder in such disorderly and frightening times people want their answers clear, clean, and easy. But it is not the task of preachers to give their people what they want, but rather to give them what they need. And clearly what the American people do not need are answers that represent a rearrangement of the facts of life, simplistic answers that inevitably lead to disenchantment. For answers that begin by explaining all too much end always by explaining all too little.

In any group of pastors there's always one who says, "I'm no great prophet; I don't take on public issues; but I'm a pretty good pastor." Every time I hear that I wince because I know it isn't true. For how can you be a good pastor and not realize how bad the Cold War is for warm Christian hearts? How can you be a good pastor without taking on the homophobia that is a thorn in the flesh of the church?

------ ⨳ ------

I want to urge the prime-time preachers, the evangelists of the so-called "electronic church," the leaders of the so-called moral majority, to "work out their salvation" with a little more "fear and trembling." I agree that the Bible contains all the answers, at least all the significant ones. But I would insist that no one understands the Bible until he has seen and lived at least part of its contents. Like any book, the Bible is something of a mirror: if an ass peers in, you can't expect an apostle to peer out!

------ ⨳ ------

What is good preaching? Good preaching is never *at* people; it's *for* people. Good preaching only raises to a conscious level the knowledge inherent in everyone's experience of life. It tells people what in their heart of hearts they already know, what in the depths of their souls they are only waiting to hear confirmed. In short, just as ears need words so do words need ears; and good preaching needs expectant people, people who yearn for something more, people who *know* there's something more, if only they could be told where to find it. Good preaching needs people who understand, as the great Russian theologian Berdyaev put it, that once bread is assured, God becomes a hard and inescapable reality, instead of an escape from harsh reality.

——— ❧ ———

The churches have to feed the hungry, clothe the naked, and shelter the homeless. But they have also to remember that the answer to homelessness is homes, not shelters. What the poor and downtrodden need is not piecemeal charity but wholesale justice.

——— ❧ ———

Every seminary graduate doesn't have to be a prophet. People need priests to stand *with* them as much as they need prophets to stand *over against* them. But "bear one another's burdens" doesn't mean being a pal to every parishioner, a minister someone once described as a "quivering mass of availability." What the second-century physician Galen said of doctors applies equally to pastors: "They heal most successfully in whom the people have the most confidence." A successful pastor is one who unveils Jesus' presence in the everyday lives of ordinary people, someone who can weave sorrow, loss, and especially death into our understanding of life.

——— ❧ ———

If evil is a soul hiding from itself, if the primary motive of evil is disguise, then we should not be surprised to find evil people in the churches. For what better way to disguise one's evil from oneself and from others than to wrap it all up in piety and to become a highly visible Christian—a preacher, let's say, or a deacon or trustee?

No two Shakespearean actors have ever sounded exactly alike, and no two readers of the Declaration of Independence, or of the Constitution of the United States, or of the sixty-six books of the Bible, will ever understand those documents in exactly the same way. Let Protestant fundamentalists claim, "The only safe interpreter of Scripture is Scripture itself." It's a fine-sounding claim, but it is pride masquerading as humility to believe that one can see so plainly revealed the mind and will of God. Search for the truth we can and must, but own it—never.

Fundamentalists are no different from the rest of us. Just as often as do we, they use a Bible as the drunk uses a lamppost: for support, not illumination. And consider this: perhaps God *approves* the struggles of the human mind to try to interpret God's designs. "The unknown is the mind's greatest need, and for it no one thinks to thank God" (Emily Dickinson). So far from being a danger to it, difference of opinion is an essential ingredient of religious life, just as difference of opinion is no danger but an essential ingredient to a healthy political life. So interpretation is not only inevitable; it's desirable.

Fundamentalists forget that love demands discernment as well as obedience.

---- ⊗ ----

Believing that all things worth knowing are already known, fundamentalist preachers create an atmosphere of cultivated ignorance which guarantees that mediocrity will be a virtue.

---- ⊗ ----

Why am I so hard on fundamentalist preachers? Because it is right to be stabbed by doubt. "Commitment is healthiest where it is not without doubt, but in spite of doubt" (Rollo May). It is wrong to be clearer than clarity warrants, to write off intellectual and moral ambiguities simply because you haven't the security to live with uncertainty. It's wrong to require certitude to the point of blind stupidity. And it is dangerous. If God is like a marine sergeant who has been handed a bunch of hopeless recruits, then those who believe in such a God will become like soldiers prepared to do almost anything they're told, no matter what, no matter to whom. To me, that is diametrically opposed to Jesus, whose central theme was that there is something intrinsically sacred, intrinsically deserving of respect, intrinsically calling for and entitled to love in every human being. Seekers of truth can build communities of love. Possessors of truth have too much enmity toward those who don't possess the truth, or possess some other truth.

Biblical inerrancy is not upheld in Scripture and belief in the inerrancy of Scripture has nothing to do with salvation. Salvation is a matter of repentance and of faith in Christ Jesus. There is no domino theory in faith. Loss of one belief doesn't lead automatically to the loss of a second; it makes the second possible with greater integrity.

------ ⸙ ------

The Christian right talks a lot about "traditional values" and "family values." Almost always these values relate to personal rather than social morality. For the Christian right has trouble not only seeing love as the core value of personal life but even more trouble seeing love as the core value of our communal life—the love that lies on the far side of justice.

------ ⸙ ------

What I hold against the religious right is its cruelty. It's cruel because it's ignorant; and as its ignorance stems from self-righteousness and complacency, it is an ethical, not an intellectual default.

------ ⸙ ------

Nothing like blind belief so fosters its opposite—blind unbelief.

------ ⸙ ------

It is absolutely right to love and learn from the books of the Bible. But it is wrong to fear their every word, for everything biblical is not Christ-like. Besides, we Christians believe in the Word made flesh, not in the Word made words. And for God's sake let's be done with the hypocrisy of claiming, "I am a biblical literalist" when everyone is a *selective* literalist, especially those who swear by the antihomosexual laws in the book of Leviticus and then feast on barbecued ribs and delight in Monday night football, for it is *toevah*, an abomination, not only to eat pork but merely to touch the skin of a dead pig.

When everything biblical is not Christ-like, we Christians need to develop an interpretive theory of Scripture. I think the love of Jesus is indeed the plumb line by which everything is to be measured. And while laws may be more rigid, love is more demanding, for love insists on motivation and goes between, around, and way beyond all laws.

The End of Life

Our times are in His hands
Who says, 'A whole I plan,'
Trust God, see all, nor be afraid.
                    —Robert Browning

God of the coming years, through paths unknown
We follow thee.
When we are strong, Lord, leave us not alone;
    Our refuge be.
Be thou for us in life our daily bread,
Our heart's true home when all our years
    have sped.
                    —Hugh Thomson Kerr

*I*t's a test of faith to grow old without resentment, free of defensiveness, to lose power without an increase in self-pity. Remember that perfectionism can apply to age as well as sin. If God can find something noble in the ruins of a life ravaged by sin, how much more noble in Her sight are lives when "crooked eclipses 'gainst its glory fight, and time that gave doth now his gift confound" (Shakespeare).

I believe in ethical elderhood. Longevity, far from a fiscal disaster, could represent the true wealth of nations if senior citizens, countering dreaded isolation, would come together to become advocates for wisdom, compassion, and the survival of the gentlest. How many people have lost their sight and thereby gained 20/20 insight? How can youth have the wealth and wisdom of accrued experience? Said Albert Camus, "To grow old is to pass from passion to compassion"— and he didn't mean compassion only for conservatives!

Memory, properly used, is like a running broad jump: it takes you back only to launch you further forward. And so the senior years ideally are the formative years. Like Abraham, who at seventy-five sought a vision, elders should look out and see and respond to the life that still needs to be protected, affirmed, dignified. If they look back, it should be primarily to remember, as did Abraham, who they were created to be—God's forgiven, cared-for, and caring co-creators of this universe.

While Abraham lived through "summer's parching heat," Jesus died young; but didn't both show us that it is by its content rather than by its duration that a lifetime is measured?

I've noticed that the older, the more gnarled the cherry tree, the greater the profusions of blossoms. And sometimes the oldest and dustiest bottles hold the most sparkling wine. I'm drawn by faces lined with crow's feet, those "credentials of humanity," beautifully lit from within.

With the severe limits that often accompany old age we are still free to choose. In fact we are never free not to choose. We are human only by our continued choices. I believe that in growing older we must carefully stake out our growing limitations in order to recognize and savor our continuing realm of freedom. Our choices may become increasingly fewer but even that can be a good thing. Until a river finds its banks it hasn't a prayer of being anything but shallow. Or to change the image, old age is like a fire threatening to destroy our home. It compels us to decide, "What do I value most?"

Without death, we'd never live. Without discovering the limits of our talents, we'd never discover who we are. And, finally, hard choices have a potential for riches beyond any reckoning, "for eye hath not seen nor ear heard nor the heart of man received the good things that God hath prepared for those who love him." Deserted by his disciples, in agony on the cross, barely thirty years old, Christ said, "It is finished." And thus ended the most complete life ever lived.

The one true freedom in life is to come to terms with death, and as early as possible, for death is an event that embraces all our lives. And the only way to have a good death is to lead a good life. Lead a good one, full of curiosity, generosity, and compassion, and there's no need at the close of the day to rage against the dying of the light. We can go gentle into that good night.

A Chinese emperor once asked a wise man to take a month off to figure out the meaning of happiness. When he returned, the wise man said, "Happiness is when the grandfather dies, then the father, and then the son."

——— ⋙ ———

Death is more friend than foe. Consider only the alternative—life without death. Life without death would be interminable—literally, figuratively. We'd take days just to get out of bed, weeks to decide "what's next?" Students would never graduate, faculty meetings and all kinds of other gatherings would go on for months. Chances are, we'd be as bored as the ancient Greek gods and up to their same mischievous tricks.

Death cannot be the enemy if it's death that brings us to life. For just as without leave-taking there can be no arrival; without growing old there can be no growing up; without tears, no laughter; so without death there can be no living.

Death also enhances our common life. Death is the great equalizer, not because it makes us equal, but because it mocks our pretensions at being anything else. In the face of death, differences of race, class, nationality, sexual orientation all become known for the trivial things they ultimately are.

Finally, with no deaths there would long since have been no births, the world being overpopulated with immortal beings. Just think: Giotto maybe, but no Cézanne, let alone Andy Warhol; Purcell maybe, but no Bach, Beethoven, Brahms, let alone Aaron Copeland; Roman gladiators yes, but no Sugar Ray Robinson or Mohammed Ali. And, of course, no you and me, no grandchildren!

——— ⋙ ———

The more we do God's will, the less unfinished business we leave behind when we die. If our lives exemplify personal charity and the pursuit of social justice, then death will not be the enemy, but rather the friendly angel leading us on to the One whose highest hope is to be able to say to each and every one of us, "Well done, thou good and faithful servant; enter into the joy of the Master."

——— ⟨⟩ ———

What in the very center of tragedy frees us for action, frees us also for gratitude. Much of course we do not understand, but all this is made bearable by the little we do understand. "The Lord gave and the Lord has taken away" does not mean God is directly responsible for every birth and every death. (Anything that makes God's love less than human love at its best has to be questioned.) What it does mean is that before every birth and after every death there is still God. He is the source and the ending, the Alpha and Omega. And if we depend radically on him, then we are free from dependent attachments to persons as to things, attachments through whom we hope to have all our longings satisfied. This means that while those we love are still alive we are free to give more than we take; and that after they die we do not have to hoard their memory but rather cherish it gratefully, be nourished by it, and go on pouring out our love to all living creatures. This is the meaning of "Let the dead bury the dead"; let the dead bury the dead and not the living.

——— ⟨⟩ ———

When our loved ones die it is not so much they whom we have lost. What are really lost are our expectations.

------ ❧ ------

We are on the road to heaven if today we walk with God. Eternal life is not a possession conferred at death; it is a present endowment. We live it now and continue it through death. With God, "time is eternity in disguise" (Heschel).

------ ❧ ------

Human life aspires beyond its grasp. As God led Moses to the mountaintop at Nebo, so life leads us to a place where we can view a land that is promised but never reached. To me, it is hard to believe a loving God would create loving creatures that aspire to be yet more loving, and then finish them off before their aspirations are complete. There must be something more.

------ ❧ ------

Of course, life after death can no more be proved than disproved. "For nothing worth proving can be proven, nor yet disproven," as Tennyson said. As a child in a womb cannot conceive of life with air and light—the very stuff of our existence—so it is hard for us to conceive of any other life without the sustaining forces to which we are accustomed. But consider this: If we are essentially spirit, not flesh; if what is substantial is intangible; if we are spirits that have bodies and not the other way around, then it makes sense that just as musicians can abandon their instruments to find others elsewhere, so at death our spirits can leave our bodies and find other forms in which to make new music.

—— ⊰≋⊱ ——

Eternal life begins not at the end of time, nor even at the funeral home, but right now; the death that comes is not the death that separates us from God. "Though he die, yet shall he live." "Whoever believes in me shall never die." St. Paul said much the same thing: "No one lives unto himself alone, and no one dies unto himself alone. If we live, we live unto the Lord; and if we die, we die unto the Lord. So whether we live or whether we die, we are the Lord's."

The abyss of God's love is deeper than the abyss of death. And she who overcomes her fear of death lives as though death were a past and not a future experience.

—— ⊰≋⊱ ——

Paul insists that "neither death nor life . . . can separate us from the love of God, which is in Christ Jesus our Lord." If death, then, is no threat to our relationship to God it should be no threat to anything. If we don't know what is beyond the grave, we do know who is beyond the grave. And Christ resurrected links the two worlds, telling us that we really live only in one. If, spiritually speaking, we die to ourselves and are resurrected in Christ, before us lies only the physical counterpart of this spiritual death. And physical death need not terrorize us, if fear of the unknown and fear of final condemnation lie behind, not before us.

—— ⟨⟩ ——

No church should ever dismiss, demean, or in any way deny the awesomeness of death, nor the fear of it that eats away at the heart of each of us, making us from time to time both insecure and militant—a lethal combination in any individual or nation. Worse yet, because our lives so often cry out for rebuke and forgiveness, we also fear that we may deserve to die. So every church worthy of the name, Sunday in and Sunday out, must proclaim the Good News that Christ is the "lamb of God that taketh away the sins of the world," that "God was in Christ reconciling the world unto itself," and yes, that there is more mercy in God than sin in us. And just as in life, so in death "nothing can separate us from the love of God." We may not know what lies beyond the grave, but we know who is there. Death is inevitable and death is awesome, but it is the fear of death that is its sting. Remove that fear, and there's not a one of us that cannot say with Paul, "O death, where is thy sting?" "O grave, where is thy victory?" What could better symbolize the defeat of death than those tombs that God caused to open up even before Christ was laid in his own!

—— ⟨⟩ ——

There is a Zen paradox whereby we may lack everything yet want for nothing. The reason is that peace, that is, deep inner peace, comes not with meeting our desires but in releasing ourselves from their power. I find such peace is increasingly mine. It's not that I feel I'm withdrawing from the world, only that I am present in a different way. I'm less intentional than "attentional." I'm more and more attentive to family and friends and to nature's beauty. Although still outraged by callous behavior, particularly in high places, I feel more often serene, grateful for God's gift of life. For the compassions that fail not, I find myself saying daily to my loving Maker, "I can no other answer make than thanks, and thanks, and ever thanks."

Also from Westminster John Knox Press

William Sloane Coffin: An American Prophet

As Seen on Public Television

DVD 0664229263
$19.95 (Canada $30.00)

VHS 0664229255
$14.95 (Canada $23.00)

Both a tribute to his remarkable life and a prophetic call to the nation, *William Sloane Coffin: An American Prophet* contains the wisdom of a man facing the end of his courageous life who has carried on a lover's quarrel with America. With powerful messages on terrorism, faith, politics, and hope—engagingly delivered as only William Sloane Coffin can—the documentary concludes with a testimony to his legacy of justice and love, given by his friends: Arthur Miller, James Carroll, Susannah Heschel, and Robert and Sally Benton.

DVD contains special features including never-before-seen interview footage with William Sloane Coffin.

Produced by Old Dog Documentaries, Inc., Copyright 2004, Westminster John Knox Press, 52 minutes, 12 seconds

---

A Passion for the Possible:
A Message to U.S. Churches
Second Edition
William Sloane Coffin
Foreword by Martin E. Marty

First published in 1993, William Sloane Coffin's *A Passion for the Possible* presents a vision for the future that challenges assumptions and deepens our understanding of the importance of social justice and change. Coffin deals with social issues that continue to face U.S. Churches—abortion, sexism, homophobia, racism, poverty, the environment, and nuclear disarmament. This second edition adds Coffin's powerful sermon preached after September 11, 2001.

0664228569
$12.95 (Canada $20.00)

Available at bookstores nationwide or at www.wjkbooks.com.